9
12/7/06

**OFFICE OF THE
'UTY PRIME MINISTER**

Searching for
Solid Foundations

Community Involvement and
Urban Policy

Gabriel Chanan, Community Development Foundation

September 2003

Office of the Deputy Prime Minister: London

Following the reorganisation of the government in May 2002, the responsibilities of the former Department for Transport, Local Government and the Regions (DTLR) in this area were transferred to the Office of the Deputy Prime Minister.

The Office of the Deputy Prime Minister
Eland House
Bressenden Place
London SW1E 5DU
Telephone 020 7944 4400
Web site www.odpm.gov.uk

Further copies of this publication are available from:

ODPM Publications
PO Box 236
Wetherby
West Yorkshire
LS23 7NB
Tel: 0870 1226 236
Fax: 0870 1226 237
Textphone: 0870 1207 405
E-mail: odpm@twoten.press.net
or online via the Office of the Deputy Prime Minister's web site.

ISBN 1 85112 660 0

Printed in Great Britain on material containing 75% post-consumer waste and 25% ECF pulp.

September 2003

Reference No. 03HC01630

Acknowledgements

Many thanks to David Rayner, Angela Ruotolo and Sarah Fielder who steered the research; to Nir Tsuk and Susan Lee who provided background material; to colleagues at the Community Development Foundation for constant stimulus and in particular to Alison West on her departure from CDF for leaps and bounds in linking community development experience to the policy arena.

CONTENTS

Chapter 5

Conclusions 81

Recommendations 90

Sources and references 92

EXECUTIVE SUMMARY

1. This research was commissioned on behalf of the Urban Policy Unit of the ODPM in mid 2002 to review government guidance on community involvement in the context of Urban Renaissance and urban policy generally.

2. Community involvement has been a growing aspect of urban policy for at least ten years, and has become particularly prominent in the last five, being a fundamental aspect of regeneration, local government modernisation and local governance. However, it occupies an ambiguous position, mostly lacking specific aims and targets. There is a tendency for community involvement objectives to get swallowed up into the objectives of other fields or to dissipate as programmes unfold.

3. In common with general usage in government literature, in this study a community is taken to mean broadly the population of a given locality. But it is recognised that in terms of common association and identity this can be an arbitrary division. There are many other forms of community, such as communities of faith, ethnicity, age, condition, that interweave with locality and must be taken into account in policies on community involvement.

4. Community involvement is therefore taken to mean certain types of activity amongst a local population, not the involvement of a unitary entity called a community.

5. Involvement is most often used to mean the involvement of local people in public decision-making. Another meaning is the involvement of people in general community activity. A third meaning is the provision of services by community and voluntary organisations.

6. A considerable volume of government guidance on community involvement has accompanied the substantial succession of new urban policies unrolled since 1998, from the expansion of regeneration schemes through Neighbourhood Renewal and Community Strategies to Urban Renaissance and local government modernisation.

7. A particular landmark of government guidance was *Involving the Community in Urban and Rural Regeneration*, produced in 1995 and revised in 1997. Other than this, most government guidance was woven into general policy documents or short pamphlets accompanying them.

8. The Urban White Paper of November 2000, which introduced Urban Renaissance, contains a particularly wide-ranging prospectus of the urban policy field, and a variety of community involvement aims can be deduced from it, namely:

    *   involvement is people's right;

    *   involvement overcomes alienation and exclusion;

    *   involvement makes the community strong in itself;

    *   involvement maximises the effectiveness of services and resources;

- involvement helps join up different conditions of development;

- involvement helps sustainability.

9. The Sustainable Communities plan of February 2003 gives a new slant to the issue of sustainable development. Community involvement was an important aspect of the widespread action on local sustainability fostered by Agenda 21 over the past ten years, but neither this nor the government's previous pronouncements on building sustainable communities squarely posed the question of what makes communities themselves sustainable. In doing so, the new plan puts community involvement as a principle high on the list, though leaves it unclear at this stage how this is intended to be operationalised.

10. The importance attached to community involvement in policies on urban development is echoed in other spheres. Examples are given from planning and health, and from the position of black and minority ethnic communities in regeneration. Another major area but not covered in detail here is housing. Tenants' and residents' associations are amongst the most basic and common vehicles for involvement, and council tenants have a right to manage.

11. Apart from a general focus on disadvantage, surprisingly few links are found between guidance on community involvement and the analytical literature on urban change. The guidance literature tends to deal with the principles of community involvement in general, assuming the existence of a community with potential to be involved, whilst the urban analysis literature shows how communities suffer from disadvantage but rarely discusses how this affects their capacity for involvement.

12. It is clear, however, that disadvantage impedes participation. A poor condition of the local community and voluntary sector is itself a component of disadvantage though rarely cited as such.

13. Some proportion of people in disadvantaged localities nevertheless struggle for improvement. Without their input, it seems impossible for action by authorities alone to arrest decline.

14. Across both advantaged and disadvantaged localities the new governance culture of partnership is beginning to work, but it is too early to say how well. People's willingness to become involved is affected by attachment to place, relations with other residents (social capital) and the openness, communicativeness and responsiveness of public authorities and partnerships.

15. Social capital is a major factor in quality of life in its own right but does not necessarily 'convert' into participation in public affairs unless the public authorities and partnerships positively seek out and foster community involvement.

16. To realise government intentions on community involvement it is necessary to move from principles and structures to strategy. Elements of such strategy already exist in various pockets of recent policies and guidance but need clearer resolution and co-ordination. Six factors in particular need clarification and development:

    (1) The strengthening of basic **social capital** underlies participation policies but is obscured by the disproportionate focus on more formal types of participation, and needs to be a policy objective in its own right.

(2) Two types of community contribution to **service provision** are often confused: (i) the devolving of parts of public services to professionalised voluntary organisations; (ii) the autonomous provision of non-statutory service by community organisations. Type (i) diversifies the provider base whilst type (ii) strengthens communities. Although sometimes mingled in complex local organisations, these are different effects requiring different treatment in policy and different streams of support.

(3) Two types of **economic value** are produced by community activity: (i) value in the cash economy, eg by job creation and small business development; and (ii) direct (non-cash) value in the reciprocal economy, eg by mutual aid and volunteering. Community enterprise as defined by government falls into the cash economy, whilst a general culture of enterprise in community activities falls into the reciprocal economy. Policy should adopt an economic model which takes account of both types. Recognising only cash value devalues the community sector and contributes to its neglect in policy.

An important hidden economic effect of community activity is that it pre-empts greater demand on statutory services. Assessing this value could help to illuminate the economic return on government investment in community development and support.

(4) **Timescales** for stages of decision-making in local development need to take account of successive waves of involvement as more remote strata of local communities gradually become involved, to avoid important decisions being sewn up before most of the community become aware that they have an opportunity to participate.

(5) **Community development** has a key role to play in creating involvement. This movement has a long tradition of relevant principles and practice, and is in the process of modernising its methods. Skilled non-directive support to multi-level community organising and involvement is the unique stock-in-trade of this discipline. But its deployment is very unstable, and as a profession it is poorly and haphazardly resourced. There is a need for better strategy and training at many levels, from neighbourhood work to strategic local planning, and for coordination of community development input from all relevant sources across a locality.

• (6) **Indicators.** One of the reasons for the lack of solidity of community involvement in policy and programmes has been the apparent lack of means for measuring it. Developing such instruments has been delayed by the fear of inappropriate or damaging criteria. However, there has been intensive development in the search for appropriate indicators in the past two years, and viable core indicators are emerging.

The report concludes by recommending that:

I   ODPM should, in consultation with the Active Communities Unit, produce a statement of the objectives of community involvement across the field of local government, housing, neighbourhood renewal and urban and regional development, drawing together the best of the principles and instruments already embedded in recent ODPM policy such as the Urban White Paper, Community Strategies, Planning reforms and the Living Places programme, and taking account of the ACU's current cross-government reviews of community capacity building and infrastructure.

This should also take account of other key issues and departments such as DEFRA to ensure the inclusion of the rural perspective, DoH on health aspects and DfES on educational aspects. This should be followed by new government guidance across the range of programmes.

II Government should promote a better understanding and appreciation of its community involvement policies and achievements in the media.

III Objectives and methods of improving community involvement at both national, regional and local level should include but clearly distinguish between:

– building up social capital and community cohesion in local communities;

– maximising local residents' engagement and involvement in public decision-making and monitoring of services;

– facilitating different types of service provision by community and voluntary organisations;

– facilitating the contribution of communities to building up local economic activity and social enterprise.

IV A clear distinction should be made between different types of service provision by community and voluntary organisations and the different criteria to be applied to them, especially distinguishing autonomous, contracted and hybrid services.

V ODPM and ACU should jointly consider the feasibility of a national review of community development and capacity building at local level.

VI Community-related programmes should include a guideline on the proportion of local budgets to be invested in community development and capacity building for community involvement, such as the 10% guideline used in the last two rounds of the Single Regeneration Budget.

VII Baselines and targets for community involvement and social capital should be considered in Neighbourhood Renewal alongside the existing floor targets.

VIII Levels of community involvement should be added to the national and regional headline sustainability indicators.

IX Research should be carried out on continuing issues of community involvement either jointly or by arrangement between the Home Office, ODPM, the Department of Health, DfES the Cabinet Office and other departments, and severally by them on departmentally specific aspects. Key issues are suggested.

X Government should press for European social policies, in particular the next period of the Structural Funds, to adopt the principles and types of method advanced in recent community involvement policies in the UK.

CHAPTER 1

Introduction

1.1 Background and purpose

Community involvement is a key aspect of urban policy. It is woven through the White Paper which introduced Urban Renaissance in 2000[1]. It is prominent in the many aspects of social policy which are drawn together and which continue to develop both separately and in concert. The 'new vision of urban living' announced in the White Paper, and progressed at the urban summit of November 2002, envisioned 'people shaping the future of their community, supported by strong and truly representative leaders'. This aim was linked with better design and planning, better use of space and buildings, more environmental sustainability, the creating and sharing of prosperity and the delivery of good quality services in health, education, housing, transport, finance, shopping, leisure and protection from crime.

The importance attached by government to community involvement can be traced through policy and guidance documents produced over a number of years, particularly in the fields of regeneration and governance. Extensive guidance in the context of regeneration was produced in 1995 and amplified in 1997[2]. The Policy Action Teams set up in 1998-9 by the Social Exclusion Unit to develop a national strategy for neighbourhood renewal placed high value on community involvement[3]. The topic is central to Community Planning and Local Strategic Partnerships; is an aspect of modernisation in all the main public services; and is a prominent principle of sustainable communities in the new plan of that name[4].

Government commitment to encouraging active communities has been clear since the establishment of the Active Community Unit in the Home Office in 1998. Community involvement is clearly a major part of, if not synonymous with, active communities, and the profile of this issue increased exponentially in the succeeding five years. Nevertheless it still occupies an ambiguous position in government policy. It is an aspect of almost every current social policy yet has few programmes or targets of its own. Its objectives are sometimes difficult to focus on because it has so many aims loosely attached to it. It is clearly fundamental to the joining up of public policies and to the whole modernisation agenda, and has spawned a copious literature over the past few years, yet there is no definitive source for government intentions on it.

---

[1] DETR (2000) *Our Towns and Cities: the Future. Delivering an Urban Renaissance.* London: ODPM (November) http://www.odpm.gov.uk.

[2] DETR (1995) *Involving Communities in Urban and Rural Regeneration.* London: ODPM. Revised edition, 1997.

[3] Fittall, W (Chair) (1999), *Report of the Policy Action Team on Community Self-Help* ('PAT 9'). London: Home Office, Active Community Unit (September).

[4] ODPM (2003) *Sustainable Communities: Building for the Future.* London: ODPM (February).

The present study was commissioned by the Office of the Deputy Prime Minister to review guidance and other literature on community involvement with particular reference to urban renaissance, and to draw out implications for the implementation of urban policy. This report therefore focuses particularly on programmes within the remit of ODPM, but takes some account of the overall government context.

Effective community involvement is a broad aim of the Government and a particular concern of the Office of the Deputy Prime Minister. The Urban White Paper states that people have a right to determine how their towns and cities develop and sets down a commitment to work with local people. Local authorities have a duty to prepare community strategies, and Local Strategic Partnerships (LSPs) are expected to engage local people in the development of community strategies in order to deliver urban policy at the local level. LSPs have to involve local people rather than just consult them.

Community involvement has been an underlying theme through different waves of regeneration policy but has had different meanings over time. Generally the focus in the past has been on encouraging participation because of a sense that it helps regeneration, rather than considering its impact on the way civil society works. More recently, initiatives such as the Single Regeneration Budget (SRB), the New Deal for Communities (NDC) and the National Strategy for Neighbourhood Renewal as a whole encourage increased community involvement. At the same time Policy Action Team 17 stressed the importance of joining up at a local level to tackle the problems of deprived neighbourhoods.

There is a need to consider the implications of the newer notions of participation at the town and city level. Government guidance on community involvement is not prescriptive, and it is not always clear how the requirement to involve the community is or should be interpreted on the ground. Encouragement of local participation can generate questions about constitution, for example, LSPs are encouraged to make decisions about budgets but this can be seen as undermining the role of elected councillors. We do not know enough about how this new level of participation impacts on governance. What does it mean for civil society? What issues does it raise? How can these be solved?

A good deal of work has already been carried out in this area by various agencies both within and outside government. Within ODPM, both the Urban Policy Unit and the Neighbourhood Renewal Unit are keen that increased community involvement leads to improvements in quality of life. The Local Government Directorate within ODPM are involved in the modernisation of local government and have commissioned an evaluation of LSPs. The Planning Division also has an interest because the Planning Green Paper emphasises the need to involve communities.

The present study aims to go beyond looking at whether community participation is useful and how to encourage it to considering its context within society and its links with the changing governance framework. These issues are broader than regeneration, though the focus of this work is particularly on implications for urban policy at the town and city level. The study concentrates on England only but draws occasionally on experience from elsewhere in the UK and Europe. It is mostly based on existing literature but also puts forward some original ideas about how the agenda can be moved forward.

Key aspects considered include:

- What is 'community'? Does it differ for different groups? What criteria can be used to define a 'community'?

- What is the meaning of involvement in this context?

- What role does the community have in achieving urban renaissance? What tensions are inherent in that role?

- What are the effects of involving the community? How does increased involvement impact on urban renaissance? What are the costs and benefits of active community involvement?

- What role does and could community development play in promoting and supporting increased community involvement?

- How do town and city bureaucratic systems help or hinder community participation? Are there obstacles in the system of governance that prevent successful involvement?

- What are the barriers preventing community involvement in achieving an urban renaissance? How can difficult to reach groups be encouraged to participate?

The rest of this chapter sets out the meaning attached here to community and community involvement.

Chapter two looks at a number of the policy 'landmarks' where community involvement has featured, tracing continuity and change in guidance from the early 1990s to urban renaissance, the 'new governance' and the further elaborations of this policy stream continuing to unroll.

Chapter three looks at what has been happening in communities: Has community involvement increased? How have the new policies interacted with economic and social change? Are there important shifts in what we now understand to be the nature of 'community' itself, and therefore the meaning and prospects for community involvement?

Chapter four looks at social capital and other aspects of community involvement where new ideas have emerged in the last five years or are needed. It also looks at recent moves to establish indicators of community involvement, and at the role and current condition of community development.

Chapter five presents conclusions and extracts some principles and recommendations to assist the realisation of the community development agenda.

The appendix details more information on indicators and lists sources and references.

1.2 What is meant by 'community'?

In many policy documents community is used in practice simply to mean 'local population'. Using 'community' instead of 'local population' adds connotations of people identifying with the place and each other, interacting with each other, helping each other and making common cause. All these are realities, but all deeper attempts to define community come to the conclusion that there are many types of community, that any one person can belong to several communities and that whatever it is that makes a group of people into a community is elusive and fluid. 'The meaning of community is most often applied to place ... Stability of residence makes for identity within a community. A powerful second element is added if place is linked with family ... Churches can also be the wellspring of organised community activities ... But there is no single model or definition of community – communities are as diverse as their members or residents, which is one of their key strengths. And any one individual may be a member of several communities, based on geography, politics, faith, social interaction, cultural interest, ethnicity.'[5]

Unfortunately this degree of fluidity about definition does not lend itself to clear policy purposes, and can lead to contradictions. Stability of residence for example may make for identity within a community of place but not necessarily in a community based on politics, faith, culture or ethnicity.

Many studies use 'community' even more loosely simply to group together a number of factors which show up at a local level. The government's strategy for sustainable development[6] lists 27 factors in 'building sustainable communities', 25 of which are simply public issues such as employment, health, transport, housing, planning and safety.

A more sophisticated definition aims to combine people and place in a balance: 'Community ... is made up of two elements: 1. Services and facilities such as housing, access to credit, goods, education, leisure activities, childcare, physical environment and transport ... 2. Social organisation such as friendship networks, group activity ... informal mutual aid, clubs and societies, and informal social controls operated via ... norms and rules'[7]

This usefully combines people and place, but seems to fly in the face of the commonsense notion that a community is primarily people, whilst public services such as goods, housing and education are not intrinsically local but just happen to be accessed locally. If we include public services and conditions of the locality in the definition of community we will find it difficult to distinguish the effects of the public services and local conditions *on* the community or, conversely, the involvement *of* the community in governance and services. We prefer therefore to attribute the primary meaning of community to *people*. What the people, conditions and services together make is the overall quality of life of the locality.

---

[5] Fittall, W (Chair), Op Cit, para 1.10ff.

[6] DETR (1999), *A Better Quality of Life. A Strategy for Sustainable Development in the United Kingdom.* London: DETR (May).

[7] Richardson, Liz and Mumford, Katharine (2002), 'Community, neighbourhood and social infrastructure' in John Hills and Julian Le Grand, eds., *Understanding Social Exclusion,* Oxford: OUP.

The Home Office study of *Measures of Community*[8] argues that what is appropriately addressed by policies on community involvement is not an entity called 'a community' but community activity amongst a given population, usually delineated by residence in a locality. Surveying a wide range of literature, the study comes to the conclusion that community *activities and attributes* amongst a given population can be meaningfully measured whereas a statement like 'Bristol is a good community' cannot.

The Library of Local Performance Indicators[9] assembles 27 examples of methods for measuring community involvement. Four of these are included in the Audit Commission 'Quality of Life' set of indicators for use by local authorities and Local Strategic Partnerships and are being tested in 2003 (see chapter four and Appendix A).

To sum up, policy documents and general discussion will no doubt continue to use 'community' to mean loosely the population of a given area, and we also adopt this commonsense meaning where appropriate; but accompanying this should be an awareness of the fluidity of the phenomenon in real conditions and a stricter usage based not on 'communities' but on community activities when we wish to make meaningful measurements.

1.3 What is meant by community involvement?

Community involvement is most often used in policy to mean the involvement of people from a given locality or a given section of the local population in public decision-making. This may mean inviting local residents as individuals to join or put forward their views to, for example, a council committee, an area forum or an LSP. Or it may mean the election or nomination of people to put forward the viewpoint of a particular grouping within the population.

A meaning less prominent in policy but more fundamental and colloquial is the involvement of people in community activities. The great majority of these activities, whether friendship groups, volunteering, sports clubs, social clubs, faith groups, carers' groups or others are not about representation or participation in council mechanisms but about the activities themselves. A proportion however are about representation in the sense of campaigning for local improvements or public causes, or representing people's interests as tenants or residents or as users of particular services. Tenants' and residents' associations are amongst the most fundamental and widespread vehicles for involvement. The general organisations may also at times be motivated to get involved in representation in order to protect their interests or further their activities.

Most of this wide undergrowth of activity is created primarily in order for people to share interests, make friends, help others, entertain, 'give something back to society'. It is not created as a whole in order to involve people in public decision-making. However, it can lend itself to some extent, to that purpose. Where it is flourishing, it is a rich source of access to local public opinion and voluntary effort.

[8] Chanan, G. (2002) *Measures of Community*. London: Home Office and Community Development Foundation (July).

[9] The Audit Commission QoL indicators were published in Sept 02 in a brochure called *Quality of Life, Public Sector Feedback Paper*, Audit Commission publications, POBox 99, Wetherby, LS23 7JA, phone 0800 502030. The full set of 27 community involvement indicators is accessible at the Library of Local Performance Indicators run jointly by the Audit Commission and IdEA at www.local-pi-library.gov.uk/index.shtml _ community involvement. The four selected for QoL (QoL 23, 24, 25, 26) are numbered there as LIB 137, 138, 139, 140.

It is less likely to flourish spontaneously under certain conditions, for example in areas with high levels of crime and harrassment, where people may distrust each other and be afraid to go out at night, or sometimes in well-off dormitory areas where people may live very individualised and seemingly self-sufficient lives.

Formal representativeness is of course embodied in the democratic machinery, and individuals can put themselves forward for election as councillors. It is widely recognised that the formal machinery is not sufficient on its own. Most council candidates are selected through political party machines which at local level may involve only a handful of activists[10] and councillors are generally elected on a minority vote. Councillors may also be felt to be more remote from local people than many community organisations are.[11] But community representatives may also have questionable legitimacy.

Whatever the condition of the local community and voluntary sector, community involvement policies seek to enlist it as the readiest source of general and varied local community effort. However, government, local authorities and other public authorities often focus on the visible surface of this activity, such as the community representatives on LSPs and neighbourhood forums, and on responses to official consultations ('vertical involvement'), without fully recognising that these expressions of local interest depend on an abundance of participation by 'average' residents in 'ordinary' community groups and networks ('horizontal' involvement).

Much of the analysis that follows turns on the relationship between these two meanings of community involvement.

---

[10] Lowndes, Vivien and others (2002), *Social Capital and Political Participation: How do Local Institutions Constrain or Enable the Mobilisation of Social capital?*. Cambridge social Capital Seminar (November).

[11] OPM (Office for Public Management) (1999), *Living in Consort and Friary Wards: A Community Survey*. London: OPM and Southwark Council.

CHAPTER 2

Policy context and guidance landmarks

2.1 The status of community involvement in the policy environment

Community involvement occupies a unique but somewhat puzzling position in current social policy. On the one hand it is a requirement accompanying virtually every policy to do with local governance and public services. On the other hand it is often vague or ambiguous in specific policy documents. Loudly trumpeted in narrative, it is often absent from listed outputs, outcomes and budget categories. Clearly signalled as central in the New Deal for Communities, Urban Renaissance, reform of the planning and health systems, Community Strategies, Local Strategic Partnerships and Neighbourhood Renewal, the element of community involvement still largely lacks the kinds of concrete targets that give clear focus and direction to policies on such issues as employment, housing, health, education and crime reduction. Community involvement is treated as having a different nature from these, somehow both larger and smaller, both over-arching and yet less solid.

For a decade and more, community involvement has been the subject of government guidance connected with specific programmes. The 1995 guidance on 'Involving Communities in Urban and Rural Regeneration', revised and extended in 1997[12] was exceptional in being a major government publication dedicated to this topic. Guidance connected with the Single Regeneration Budget, New Deal for Communities, Urban Renaissance, the National Strategy for Neighbourhood Renewal and programmes in planning, childcare, health, education, housing and other issues has mostly been incorporated into broader guidance on the operation of those programmes as a whole.

For community involvement to become established in policy in more visible and analysable ways it would be necessary to have distinct components of programmes clearly dedicated to it, and measures for its achievement and effectiveness. Some factors that would make this possible have recently emerged. The Active Community Unit of the Home Office is carrying out cross-cutting reviews of community capacity building and community and voluntary sector infrastructure. The first biennial national citizenship survey[13] provides some benchmarks for 'active citizenship'. The Audit Commission has added items on community involvement into its Quality of Life indicators for local authorities and Local Strategic Partnerships[14]. The Treasury cross-cutting review of

---

[12] DETR (1997), *Involving Communities in Urban and Rural Regeneration*. London: ODPM.

[13] Duncan Prime and others, *Active Communities: Initial Findings from the 2001 Home Office Citizenship Survey*. London: Home Office (Research, Development and Statistics Department) 2002 (April).

[14] Audit Commission, *Quality of Life, Using Quality of Life Indicators, Public Sector Feedback Paper*. Wetherby: Audit Commission Publications, 2002 (Oct).

'The role of the voluntary and community sector in service delivery'[15] introduces a programme of capacity building for voluntary and community sector involvement in service delivery. And ideas on social capital have been circulating in government since the publication of a review on this subject by the Performance and Innovation (now Strategy) Unit in April 2002[16].

These developments are both promising and worrying. Promising because clear policy objectives for community involvement would be a major step forward in deepening democratic practice and forging a new kind of understanding between state and citizens. Worrying because there is a legacy of unfulfilled aspirations in this field. Community involvement objectives tend to get swallowed up into the objectives of other fields or disappear from view as programmes unfold.

The present report charts some of the main factors affecting the prospects for establishing community involvement as a distinct and demonstrable feature of social policy. This chapter reviews some of the main landmarks in government and related guidance on community involvement to date.

2.2 The emergence of community involvement as a policy issue

Regeneration and urban renewal of one kind or another have been the main vehicles for government's community involvement intentions since the 1960s. 'Modern' regeneration in the UK could be said to have begun with City Challenge in the early 1990s, which challenged local authorities both on the quality of their regeneration plans and their ability to involve local residents.

City Challenge aimed to overcome the limitations of earlier approaches to urban renewal. Assessing the impact of urban policy between 1980 and 1990, Brian Robson and others[17] found a moderate degree of success in terms of economic criteria and benefits for localities but nevertheless a widening gap between the most and least disadvantaged residents. One of its conclusions was that there was a need for much more involvement, 'Benefits appear to have had as much or more effect on the broader surrounding areas as on the targeted areas themselves ... (This) adds force to the need to develop effective linkages between policy targeted at areas and the disadvantaged residents living in those areas ... (There is) scope to capitalise on the place-loyalty of local communities ... The evidence of increasing polarisation offers strong arguments for the community sector having access to some form of programme which addresses the need to strengthen the capacities of deprived communities ... Effective coalitions within localities ... require long-term collaborative partnerships ... Local communities need to be given opportunities to play roles in such coalitions.'[18]

---

15 HM Treasury, *The Role of the Voluntary and Community Sector in Service Delivery*. London: HM Treasury, 2002 (Sept).

16 PIU (Later Strategy Unit) (2002) *Social Capital, A Discussion Paper*. London: Cabinet Office.

17 Robson, Brian and others (1994) *Assessing the Impact of Urban Policy*. London: HMSO.

18 Ibid, Summary, pp x-xiv.

There was already by this time a considerable history of attempts to involve communities in public policy, particularly around tenant participation and local authority decentralisation experiments. In the background was the original European poverty programme of the early 1990s, which made participation a high priority but gave no clear definition of it. Evaluation of this aspect was therefore inconclusive. Only four out of the 41 projects carried out across the EU recorded the number of local voluntary or community organisations supported by their actions. 'The largest group of projects felt that the direct participation of target groups ... was problematic ... Some felt that participation was practically impossible to make viable' though one project reported that 'the decision to work with local associations was the key which opened the door to involving the target groups ... This allowed the concept of participation to develop bit by bit into the realms of planning and executing actions'.[19]

City Challenge ran from 1992 to 1998. During this time the much larger Urban Programme was phased out and the Single Regeneration Budget was begun. City Challenge was a substantial concentration of resources on a small number of deprived areas. Each of 31 partnerships received £37.5m over five years. The aims included promoting successful partnerships of public, private and voluntary bodies and local communities; and developing capacity within the targeted neighbourhoods for self-sustaining regeneration and self help. 'Players saw it as an improvement on previous regeneration initiatives particularly ... because of community and private sector involvement'[20]. 'Left to themselves, developers (in both the private and public sectors) have produced poorly conceived, poorly designed, poorly built environments, and have shown no awareness of the interrelationships between economic, housing and social policies. Local people are being introduced into the development process because, as the intended beneficiaries ... they have the greatest stake in the future of the area, and they know from experience the range of issues ...' [21]

The most widespread understanding of community involvement at this time was that it meant consultation with local residents, either through public meetings and surveys, or through the good offices of local voluntary sector umbrella groups. There were also specific mechanisms to promote involvement in particular policy area, such as the right to manage for council tenants, introduced in 1993, allowed Tenant Management Organisations (TMOs) to take on responsibility for a varying range of management and maintenance services[22]. More radically, the idea of a 'ladder of participation', stretching from merely being informed through being consulted to complete control and delivery of public services had been in circulation since 1969.[23] The higher rungs of the ladder were never in much danger of being put to the test, but the basically simple concept proved extraordinarily durable (how many journal articles are still widely quoted over thirty years later?). The ladder metaphor however has two drawbacks. It implies that 'the community' as a whole could move up this tariff, whereas in practice certain people and organisations

[19] Animation and Research (1994). *Poverty 3, Developments and Achievements. Central Unit Report, Fourth period.* Lille: EEIG Animation and Research, p160-1.

[20] KPMG (1998) *Final evaluation of City Challenge: What works – emerging lessons for urban regeneration.* London: DETR, (February), p3.

[21] MacFarlane, Richard (1993) *Community Involvement in City Challenge, A Policy Report,* London: National Council for Voluntary Organisations.

[22] ODPM (2002) *Tenants managing: evaluation of TMOS in England,* Housing Research Summary number 174. www.odpm.gov.uk/housing Then follow path Housing research >housing research summaries> 2002

[23] Arnstein, S. (1969) 'A ladder of citizen participation in the USA', *Journal of the American Institute of Planners,* July 1969.

might move up it whilst the majority remain uninvolved and unaware. It also tends to perpetuate the dubious conception that delivery of services by communities would be the ultimate form of involvement. Having influence and control is undoubtedly a higher level of involvement than being informed and consulted, but managing and delivering public services is a different thing altogether. We look more closely at this issue in discussing the Treasury review at the end of this chapter.

2.3 Fluctuations

Two years into City Challenge, an independent evaluation by the National Council for Voluntary Organisations found 'a growing involvement of local communities in project implementation ...(but) it is patchy ... it takes time for communities to get organised and ... it requires a commitment to openness, flexibility and innovation by all partners [which is often lacking]'[24]. The evaluation admitted that it was too early to attempt a full assessment of the impact of community involvement, but feared that 'under the existing evaluation criteria none of the advantages of community involvement ... will be adequately assessed' (p39). Despite this timely alert, the prediction was borne out. The issue of community involvement was barely visible in the final evaluation of City Challenge commissioned by DETR[25]. The omission is difficult to explain, given the clear inclusion of community involvement in the basic objectives, but alas it is only one of a number of examples of 'the disappearing community' in policy and programme trajectories.

The commencement of the Single Regeneration Budget (SRB) in England in 1994 raised the sights of involvement to include 'involving the community in setting up and running these programmes'. The platform was still mainly consultation but 'intended beneficiaries' were expected to 'have a continuing say in the management, further development and implementation of the scheme'[26].

At first community involvement in SRB remained, as in City Challenge, mainly an exhortation rather than part of the structure of criteria, outputs and budgets. The fifth of the six rounds momentously introduced capacity building of the community sector as a virtually obligatory output using up to 10% of the grant. The definition of capacity-building oscillated somewhat between on the one hand building up the community and voluntary sector in general and on the other hand, merely training and supporting community representatives[27]. This substantial earmarking of resources for community involvement now looks vulnerable again with the ending of SRB and the transfer of its remaining resources to a 'single pot' in Regional Development Agencies.

Whilst continuing to unroll the SRB regime which it had inherited from the preceding government, New Labour created an additional variant, the New Deal for Communities (NDC), in which local residents were given a clear central role. 'The new programme will support plans that bring together local people, community and voluntary organisations, public agencies, local authorities and business in an intensive local focus to tackle these problems (jobs, crime, environment, neighbourhood management) and make a lasting

---

[24] MacFarlane, op cit, p37.

[25] KPMG, op cit.

[26] *SRB Challenge Fund, Guidance Note 1*. London DoE (later ODPM) 1995.

[27] DETR (1998), *Single Regeneration Budget Bidding Guidance Round 5*. London: ODPM.

improvement'[28]. Participation was closely linked with an unprecedented flexibility of aims: 'The key to the New Deal for Communities is that it is flexible and very local. There will be complete flexibility on what programmes can cover; bodies such as housing associations, the private sector and voluntary organisations will be given the chance to lead regeneration programmes, and the very local focus will allow communities to identify closely with the programme and be actively involved ... Partnerships will be expected to involve the whole community throughout the process, secure their participation, listen to and act on their views and gain their support. Experience shows that solutions which are imposed on a community rather than developed with them won't deliver lasting change' (p2).

These principles might have been expected to apply to the whole of the emerging National Strategy for Neighbourhood Renewal, of which NDC was the first fruit, but when the full strategy emerged (see below) flexibility was firmly de-linked by the setting of 'floor targets' on employment, health, housing, safety and education. The principle of involvement was clearly retained but may have suffered some 'constructive demotion' by the dominance of the floor targets. We comment on this dilemma in chapter five.

2.4   Guidance landmarks

During the SRB period leading up to NDC, the DETR produced guidance which played a major role in moving community involvement from aspiration to practice in regeneration schemes. *Involving Communities in Urban and Rural Regeneration*[29] addressed both the underlying philosophy of involvement and the practicalities. Echoing the 'ladder of participation' concept, it defined community involvement as 'any effort to involve the community in regeneration, from informing people of what decisions have been made and what is planned, through to delegating full decision-making powers and responsibility for expenditure to a community organisation to deliver some element – or the totality – of a regeneration programme'.[30] Drawing on a now considerable literature in the field, and illustrating its approach with numerous brief summaries of successful practice emerging from existing schemes, it defined principles of involvement and how to implement it by stages from building partnerships, through involvement in the bid process, design and management of projects, to monitoring and forward strategies, and how to work with particular sections of the community. The revised edition, in 1997, added guidance on involving ethnic minorities, faith communities and young people.

Involving Communities is a storehouse of still relevant and valuable advice, and is presented in a way which flows easily into the subsequent frameworks of community strategies and neighbourhood renewal. However, as in much other literature, community involvement is mostly seen from the 'top-down' point of view: 'The purpose of this manual is to provide advice to those responsible for regeneration activity at the local level on how to set about involving the community'(1.2); '...Identify the different interests within a community which the partnership wishes to involve' (4.2).

[28] DETR (1998). *New Deal for Communities Phase 1 Proposals, Guidance for Pathfinder Applicants*. London: DETR (September), p1.

[29] DETR (1995, revised 1997) *Involving Communities in Urban and Rural Regeneration*. London: ODPM.

[30] Ibid, p10.

Parallel ideas were included in the local government modernisation agenda. Research commissioned to guide public involvement in the modernisation of local government[31] focussed largely on how to change the culture of the local authority rather than how to build up the culture of the community, though it included recognition of the need to build capacity and of the range of obstacles facing people who might want to become involved. Local authorities were urged to adopt a systematic approach to involvement consisting of four elements: improved comprehension of what local authorities do; better communication within themselves and with the public; developing capacity, again both within the authority and 'to encourage non-joiners among the public and build a better civic infrastructure'; and strengthening connections, again both across the authority and in partnerships (p40). Obstacles to be overcome were: rural distances; frail elderly; women with continuous care commitments; disability; language and cultural barriers; alienation amongst young people; lack of skills. 'There is an argument for each authority to consider the potential role of community development and youth work in supporting and enabling the involvement of a wider range of people ... there is also the potential of citizenship education' (p35).

However, unusually, there was also frank realism about the possibility of ever having a total unity of perspective between public authorities and local residents: 'Engaging with the public has become a touchstone for the general effectiveness of local authorities ... A key ... is to recognise the gap between official perspectives on participation and the public's view. There is a gap and it will never be fully closed, reflecting as it does the inevitable distance, the 'us and them' dimension, to relations between government and people ...' (p6). 'Each time a policy is proposed or a service assessed the question should be asked *What does the public think?* Equally, knowing more about the public's view does not determine the decision. Evidence of public opinion is often unclear, contradictory or slanted. Councillors have a key role in judging the strengths and weaknesses of the public's view' (p37).

At this time the recently established Social Exclusion Unit of the Cabinet Office was pulling together the best ideas it could find on every topic that might have a bearing on social exclusion. The 18 'Policy Action Teams' (PATs) on social exclusion would soon lead to the National Strategy for Neighbourhood Renewal, an unprecedentedly concentrated programme to overcome disadvantage.

The PAT report on 'community self-help'[32] articulated a fuller concept of the crucial relationship between community involvement in public affairs and the inner dynamics of the community itself: 'Self-help is an end in itself, as well as a means to an end. It is at the core of the empowerment of communities ... about involvement and consultation but also about moving towards self sufficiency... about communities shaping their own destiny – doing, not being done to' (1.3).

However, it may be that in emphasising self-help, the 'PAT 9' report underestimated the need for community development assistance. Some at least of the twenty capsule case studies of community self-help which it included would almost certainly have been stimulated or assisted by a community worker who remains invisible:

---

[31] Lowndes, Vivien and others (1998), *Modern Local Government: Guidance on Enhancing Public Participation.* London: DETR (October).

[32] Fittall, William (Chair) (1999), *Report of the Policy Action Team on Community Self-Help*, ('PAT 9'). London: Home Ofice, Active Community Unit, (April).

- a group of single parent families in a housing estate in West Glamorgan who started by meeting socially and ended up running a youth club;

- a group of residents in a village near Bath who took over its threatened grocery store and ran it on a self-help basis;

- members of a residents' association in Hillingdon who turned a neglected piece of derelict land into allotments and a wildlife area under their own management;

- a group of women who set up a child-sharing rota to enable some of them to go back to college, and it became a community co-operative which then gained the contract for the college crèche;

- an embroidery group set up by Asian women in East London which became a tailoring co-operative and gained contracts from the garment trade.

It is characteristic of community development method for the element of professional help to be non-directive and self-effacing, precisely in order to enable the residents to take the reins. But in a policy document this has, ironically, the effect of concealing the extent of the need for community development input to build up community groups, organisations and networks. We look at the contribution and the current condition of community development practice at the end of chapter four.

2.5 Urban Renaissance – a crystallisation of key policies

The Urban White Paper of November 2000, *Our Towns and Cities: The Future*, was an exceptionally 'joined up' expression of social policy. It articulated in a co-ordinated way the essential aims of community strategies, neighbourhood renewal and the continuing regeneration programmes. It combined commitments to overcoming poverty, promoting prosperity, achieving better public service through higher investment coupled with clear targets, reduction of competing policy initiatives and support for community involvement to meet a range of purposes connected with these aims.

Seen through the prism of this document, New Labour's social policy looked coherent and comprehensive. But three years on, the White Paper is in danger of becoming something of an unread classic. It has proved difficult for people tasked with implementing one or another specific part of the policy, whether at government, local government or community level, to keep in mind the whole pattern.

Community involvement was a frequent topic in the debate leading up to the Urban White Paper but was rarely approached strategically. The 'Urban Task Force'[33] which paved the way for the Urban White Paper took on the task of identifying causes of urban decline in England and recommending practical solutions to bring people back into cities, towns and urban neighbourhoods. It aimed to establish a new vision for urban regeneration founded on the principles of design excellence, social well-being and environmental responsibility within a viable economic and legislative framework.

---

[33] DETR (June) Rogers of Riverside, Lord (Chair) (1999) *Towards an Urban Renaissance, Report of the Urban Task Force*. (Executive summary.) London: ODPM.

Key themes were: recycling land and buildings, improving the urban environment, achieving excellence in leadership, participation and management, and delivering regeneration. Community involvement was largely subsumed within 'achieving excellence' in such forms as devolving detailed planning to the level of the neighbourhood where local people could get more involved in decision-making, and establishing a fund for local groups to improve their own neighbourhoods.

The report also recommended piloting different models of neighbourhood management that would give local people a stake in the decision-making process.

How does community involvement feature in the Urban White Paper itself? It is woven into the narrative prominently at the beginning and then again at a number of other points without an overall definition or intention being pulled together. It is not difficult however to gather the implied meanings and purposes attached to it. Six principles or purposes of involvement can be distinguished:

(A). ***Involvement is people's right***: 'People have a right to determine their future and be involved in deciding how their town or city develops … It is not enough to consult people … they must be fully engaged in the process from the start and … everybody must be included' (p32, Para 3.10).

(B). ***Involvement overcomes alienation and exclusion***: 'Local authorities need to engage local communities. Too often local people feel powerless to influence what happens in their community. They are daunted by, or alienated from, officialdom … We want to change this' (p33, 3.13). 'We want all who live in urban areas to have the opportunity to achieve their full potential, regardless of … race, age, gender, faith or disability' (p36, 3.35).

(C). ***Involvement makes the community stronger in itself***: '(We intend) equipping people to participate in developing their communities' (p8); '(We want) 'councils that listen to, lead and build up their local communities' (p32, 3.11); 'We are also seeking to increase community activity and volunteering through our new active community programme' (p110, 6.26).

(D). ***Involvement maximises the effectiveness of services and resources***: 'We need local strategies developed with local people to meet the needs of local people… voluntary organisations and other service providers with the common objective of improving quality of life' (p32, 3.11). 'Without real commitment from the community we will not be able to make the best use of the resources available' (p33, 3.13).

(E). ***Involvement helps 'join-up' different contributions to development***: 'Establishing a framework for effective partnerships to allow properly joined up strategies to be developed and implemented with local people and all the organisations involved in tackling local problems' (p31, 3.1).

(F). ***Involvement helps sustainability***: 'A clear message from the regeneration initiatives of the last 30 years is that real sustainable change will not be achieved unless local people are in the driving seat' (p32, 3.10); 'Key to ensuring long term sustainable change is to involve the local community, the people who live and work in an area' (p108, 6.25).

These purposes can be summarised as reflecting an essential 'triangle' of mutually enhancing objectives:

- involvement as **governance** (A, E, F);

- involvement as **social capital** (B, C);

- involvement as **service delivery** (D).

The White Paper has much to say about creating a culture of enterprise but little about community enterprise in the sense in which it had been defined by government the year before,[34] as a specific form of commercial activity. This might have formed a link between community involvement and economic development, an issue we discuss in chapter four below. In terms of this framework community enterprise as a commercial activity could be seen as a form of service delivery, but perhaps should be added as a distinct fourth element, whilst community enterprise as the general initiative to get things done in communities would be a form of social capital.

The six purposes of community involvement woven into the White Paper are perhaps the nearest thing to a comprehensive framework for government intentions on community involvement. This is not to say that they are necessarily comprehensive. We return to these in chapter five.

2.6 Neighbourhood Renewal, Community Strategies and LSPs

The Urban White Paper was rapidly followed by guidance on Community Strategies and Local Strategic Partnerships, and the Neighbourhood Renewal action plan[35]. The aim of community strategies was stated[36] as being to enhance the quality of life of local communities and contribute to the achievement of sustainable development in the UK. 'Allowing local communities (based on geography and/or interest) to articulate their aspirations, needs and priorities' (para 11) is the first of four objectives, and partnerships are exhorted to 'ensure that community and voluntary organisations are in a position to play a full and equal part in multi-agency partnerships' (para 47).

The National Strategy for Neighbourhood Renewal was announced as marking the beginning of a new approach to turning round the most deprived communities. Neighbourhood decline was attributed to economic change, the decline of old industries, joblessness, family breakdown, the decline of social housing and 'ever greater concentration of vulnerable people in poor neighbourhoods... Government policies have not been good enough at tackling these issues and sometimes they have been part of the problem... Government failed to harness the knowledge and energy of local people or empower them to develop their own solutions' (p7).

[34] DETR (1999) *Community Enterprise Good Practice Guide*. London: DETR (May).

[35] Social Exclusion Unit (2001), *A New Commitment to Neighbourhood Renewal, National Strategy Action Plan*. London: Cabinet Office, SEU (January).

[36] DETR (2000), *Preparing Community Strategies, Government Guidance to Local Authorities*. London: ODPM (December).

The strategy aimed to initiate a long-term process to ensure that within 10 to 20 years, no-one would be seriously disadvantaged by where they lived. There were three key dimensions: new policies, funding and targets; better local co-ordination and community empowerment; and national and regional support' (p8). There followed what rapidly became known as the 'floor targets' ('Whitehall departments will be judged for the first time on the areas where they are doing worst rather than on the national average') in work and enterprise, crime, education and skills, health, housing and physical environment' (p9-10). Mechanisms for empowering communities would include Local Strategic Partnerships, neighbourhood management pathfinders ('someone visibly taking responsibility at the sharp end'), the Community Empowerment Fund to help communities participate in LSPs, and Community Chests 'to fund local small grant schemes so that communities can run their own projects' (p10). Resources were targeted at the 88 local authorities containing the most deprived neighbourhoods, but the principles were commended to all local authorities.

An agenda of 105 'government commitments to help realise this long-term vision' was assembled (p61ff). These covered the local economy, health, housing, crime, education and community involvement. Twelve of the 105 commitments were directly relevant to community involvement:

- Community Development Venture Fund (Commitment 7)

- Innovation fund, to support community and voluntary organisations linking people with employment (23)

- Establishment of 6000 UK Online centres. Every deprived area to have at least one accessible, community-based facility (43)

- A small fund to enable local authorities to boost tenant participation (70)

- NR strategies and LSPs to be judged by government regional offices partly on the degree of resident involvement (84)

- Requirement on LSPs to seek out as well as welcome resident involvement (89)

- Community Empowerment Fund (90)[37]

- Support for faith organisations (91)

- A community task force to advise the NRU on how communities priorities and needs can best be met (92)

- Community chests (93)[38]

- Simplified access to funding for community groups (94)

- Clear responsibility to ensure that neighborhood renewal benefits ethnic minorities (98).

---

[37] DTLR Neighbourhood Renewal Unit (2001), *Community Empowerment Fund, Preliminary Guidance.* London: ODPM.

[38] DTLR Neighbourhood Renewal Unit (2001), *Neighbourhood Renewal Community Chests.* London: ODPM.

These amounted to by far the most concerted effort by government yet seen to turn community involvement aspirations into concrete reality. Pointers to how to put these into practice were more cryptic, and focussed mainly on the visible pinnacle of involvement, ie the LSP: 'Community involvement is a complex process and to do it well would include at least the following steps:

- outreach, especially to excluded communities, to make them aware they have the chance to express their views and influence service providers;

- facilitation to pull together the community's views and procedures for choosing community members of the LSPs;

- participation of community members in sufficient numbers on the LSP, for which they might need training and other forms of support;

- Government Office action if an LSP does not enagage with the community appropriately' (p52).

– adding however that many of these issues needed to be approached at neighbourhood level.

The guidance on Local Strategic Partnerships[39] is perhaps the clearest of all the New Labour policy documents on the subject of how community involvement might be achieved: 'In response to views expressed during consultation the revised guidance emphasises even more strongly … the importance of involving local people. Partnerships will not succeed unless they provide real opportunities for people to express their views, influence decisions and play an active part in shaping the future of their communities. Special efforts must be made to involve groups that might otherwise be hard to reach, including faith, black and minority ethnic communities' (p5, Preface by Hilary Armstrong).

The guidance urges attention at an early stage to ensuring that local communities are given the support they need to participate fully. 'In addition to membership of the partnership itself, a variety of methods may be successful including:

- feeding in local people's views through other partnerships with narrower remits;

- direct consultation;

- ensuring openness and transparency by making information easily accessible;

- capacity building and training to enhance the involvement of hard to reach communities;

- recognition of the need to facilitate greater levels of participation … at local level.'

LSPs are expected to draw on existing community networks and to build on the government compact with the voluntary and community sector.[40]

[39] DETR (2001), *Local Strategic Partnerships, Government Guidance*. London: ODPM (March).

[40] Home Office (1998), *Compact on Relations between Government and the Voluntary and Community Sectors in England.* London: Home Office (November).

Whilst the early sections stress the notion of the community as an 'untapped pool of resources' (para 1.19) Annex C recognises that the community contribution depends on the condition of the community in a particular place. 'The level of community and voluntary actvity in an area is often a gauge of the social health and spirit of that area and as such is a vital complementary strand to the provision of decent public services and a quality environment in changing people's lives. LSPs should therefore ensure that community and voluntary organisations and local people more widely are in a position to play a full and equal part in multi-agency partnerships' (Annex C, para 12, p58).

The same Annex then articulates a crucial distinction between two of the purposes that had been covered in the Urban White Paper but which are often confused elsewhere in both government and non-government literature: 'There are two quite different ways in which people working in community and voluntary sector groups might be involved in an LSP. The first category relates to their role in providing services for their own members and for other local people and the second category relates to their role in speaking for local people' (Annex C paras 13-14).

These principles were echoed in the guidance which Government Offices of the Regions were intended to apply in accrediting the new LSPs in the 88 local authority areas eligible to draw down Neighbourhood Renewal Fund[41]. LSPs were to:

(a) be effective, representative and capable of playing a key strategic role;

(b) actively involve all the key players, including the public, private, community and voluntary sectors;

(c) establish genuine common priorities and targets, agreed actions and milestones leading to demonstrable improvements;

(d) ensure that member organisations aligned their... management, aims, objectives and processes to the LSP;

(e) reduce, not add to, the bureaucratic burden; and

(f) build on best practice. (Section 3)

In working with the community and voluntary sectors the LSP should also be sure to bring in black and minority ethnic communities, take account of the compact and its further development, and make use of recognised community networks to be supported by the Neighbourhood Renewal Unit.

In the event, however, the first round of LSPs were virtually accredited *en bloc*.

The LSP and Community Strategies guidance also refers to other guidance on community involvement available from the Community Development Foundation. CDF had been producing guidance on this subject supplementary to government policy since the beginning of the Single Regeneration Budget. This distinguished five different roles for communities that should guide different aspects of practice and different criteria of success:

---

[41] DTLR (October), Neighbourhood Renewal Unit (2001) *Accreditation Guidance for Local Strategic Partnerships*. London.

- as beneficiaries of programmes and users of services;

- as consultees and representatives of local opinion;

- as a source of general community activity;

- as a source of organisations which could help to deliver parts of the regeneration programme; and

- as potential long-term partners in regeneration.[42]

In relation to the Community Strategies[43] CDF emphasised that an increasing involvement of people 'upwards' into development plans would depend on first increasing their involvement 'outwards' into general community activity: 'A strategy for strengthening communities should... address first and foremost people's ability to relate to *each other*' (p16); and recommended maintaining clear distinctions between:

- activity which represents the community, as users and controllers;

- activity which the community freely chooses to do (or to stop doing) for itself, eg mutual aid; and

- activity which bids to deliver some part of the public services by taking on a contract and the systematic accountability that goes with it (p19).

In a handbook on community involvement in a European context[44] CDF proposed that the metaphor of a ladder of involvement should be replaced by a pyramid, which would allow for the fact that the ability of a small number of residents to get involved 'vertically' in decision-making arenas such as the LSP depended on the ability of the mass of local residents to get involved at a variety of levels 'horizontally' in general community activity.

Despite its centrality in Neighbourhood Renewal, Community Strategies and the Urban White Paper, community involvement seems to dwindle to the margins again in the White Paper on local authority leadership in December 2001[45], and alarmingly, the Urban White Paper's own implementation plan[46] appeared to forget community involvement altogether. In the Urban Summit of November 2002, scheduled to check progress made in the two years since the launch of the Urban White Paper, housing, planning and economic development were naturally prominent. The Deputy Prime Minister heralded the development of the sustainable communities plan (see below) which would be designed to ensure that new planning and building produced not just houses and estates but communities. The Chancellor emphasised the role of community and voluntary

[42] Community Development Foundation (1997), *Guidelines to the Community Involvement Aspect of the SRB Challenge Fund, 1997 Edition*. London: CDF (April).

[43] Chanan, G., Garratt, C. and West, A. (2000), *The New Community Strategies, How to Involve Local People*. London: CDF.

[44] Chanan, G. (1999), *Local Community Involvement, A Guide to Good Practice*. Dublin: European Foundation for the Improvement of Living and Working Conditions.

[45] DTLR (2001), *Strong Local Leadership, Quality Public Services*. London: ODPM.

[46] DETR (2001), *Our Towns and Cities: The Future, Implementation Plan*. London: ODPM.

organisations in overcoming poverty and worklessness, and drew on the lately produced Treasury cross-cutting report[47] setting out a programme and resources for boosting the role of the voluntary and community sector in service delivery. The theme of community involvement however remained shadowy.

2.7 The role of the community in service delivery – the Treasury review

Accompanied by a detailed programme of government action and backed with resources, the cross-cutting review embodied a new stage in linking government involvement in the voluntary and community sector across issues and departments. The review set out a detailed plan for co-ordinating national action on capacity building, led by the Active Community Unit. As the remit makes clear, the subject is the sector's service delivery role. Nevertheless, the approach is informed by a sense of the interconnections between the service-delivery function and the strength of the sector as a whole. The opening sentences are about community involvement and, curiously perhaps, no distinct reasons are given as to why there is a commitment to boost the sector's service delivery role. The Prime Minister, interviewed on radio[48], put the voluntary sector service delivery role into the context of general new flexibility in delivery of public services ('a trend all over the world'), which appeared to imply that the reasoning was about getting services delivered more cheaply and cost-effectively. But boosting the sector role clearly also takes much of its moral force from some unspoken connection with community involvement as a whole.

The review gives striking evidence on the skewed distribution of resources as between community organisations and professionally-led voluntary organisations, but draws no conclusions from this. It does however frequently invoke 'the voluntary and community sector' and use 'VCOs' (voluntary and community organisations) throughout, suggesting that the role of the community sector should be fully asserted within this framework.

The Treasury review skirts round some longstanding dilemmas: does *more volunteering* equate with *more active communities*? Does capacity building *to deliver services* strengthen *community involvement*? Are the mutual-aid activities of small community groups a form of *service*? Does the huge disproportion of financial resources between the 'leading' voluntary sector organisations and the mass of local community organisations inhibit service delivery and involvement, or is it simply a natural concomitant of different roles in different parts of the sector?

An understanding of the difference between professionally-led voluntary organisations on the one hand and community organisations on the other is crucial to any realistic understanding of the sector. There has been much debate about whether the community sector and voluntary sector are two parts of the same sector or are separate sectors. Technically and legally there is much overlap but it can easily be seen that there is an extreme divergence in size, function and ethos between the larger and professionally staffed voluntary organisations and the (much larger number of) small community-led organisations. One obvious difference is that the great majority of community

---

[47] *The Role of the Voluntary and Community Sector in Service Delivery.* London: H M Treasury, 2002 (Sept).

[48] 'Today', BBC Radio 4, 3 Oct 2002.

organisations have very little funding or paid staffing – four fifths have no paid staff at all.[49] Nevertheless, there is continuity along the spectrum and there are a number of organisations which clearly share characteristics of both types. Indeed, some of the most important community organisations are those which have grown to take on staff and formal service commitments without losing their community ethos and accountability.

This is not merely a matter of degree but of major differences in purpose. Community organisations embody and exercise community capacity autonomously and to that extent represent some part of the community. Professional voluntary organisations serve the community and may also mobilise help from it, but are ultimately accountable to the terms of contracts or their specialist ethos and so are not community-driven, though some may have started out that way.

In practice the Treasury review appears to endorse the distinction made in the LSP guidance between providing services and speaking for local people. The implementation plan at the end of the Treasury Review is more balanced as between the two parts of the sector than the central text. 18 of the 42 practical recommendations need community involvement (recommendations 1, 3, 4, 5, 6, 7, 8, 9, 11, 26, 27, 28, 29, 30, 37, 38, 39, 41, 42). Many of these are not about service delivery but about involvement in service *planning and monitoring,* and it is recognised that community groups need capacity building for this role not just for service delivery. In chapter five below we take up the vital question of how far the objectives of community involvement can be covered by policies on service delivery.

2.8 Living places and sustainable communities

The physical side of local community conditions was addressed in the government's 'Living Places' policy published in October 2002.[50] Spanning community involvement and local environmental conditions, this policy on the one hand highlights the effect of local space on quality of life and on the other, seeks to enlist residents' active engagement in looking after and improving that space: 'Engaging people in schemes that improve the quality of the places where they live or work can range from the clean-up of a local pond to the pedestrianisation of Trafalgar Square… The benefits of active involvement of local people can outweigh the additional efforts required – active engagement of the community has been proven to bring about results that better meet users' needs. Where communities have been effectively engaged in projects the outcomes are better – and stay that way for longer. This has been shown time and time again' (p15).

The value of this involvement is seen not merely as supplementing public services. The additional value of building social capital is also recognised: 'Moreover there are important benefits for local people themselves from being involved in community activity – the opportunities for meeting and working closely with other local people, for developing new skills and for building confidence that can lead to greater community cohesion. Increasingly these are being recognised and efforts are being made to build community involvement into all stages of policy and action' (p15).

[49] National Council for Voluntary Organisations, *Research Quarterly No 2*. London: NCVO, 1998 (June).

[50] ODPM (2002) *Living Places – Cleaner, Safer, Greener.* London: ODPM (October).

Thus *Living Places* implicitly raises the question of whether genuine social capital can be built through a state scheme to mobilise people to support public services. Does this amount to autonomous community activity or is it merely the drafting of volunteers to back up state provision? Looking after local open space is an interesting frontier, it is an issue on which people are often highly motivated to take action close to home, yet where they may be thwarted by the fact that public space is controlled by authorities and therefore subject to much regulation and formal decision-making. Here then is an issue where 'handing over control to the local community' would seem particularly apt. But groups of activists are never synonymous with the whole community. How can public assets be handed over to self-appointed groups without some safeguard of the wider public interest?

Living Places comes up with a scheme called 'community enablers'[51] which on the one hand deploys practical help to community groups who may want to take on the improvement of their local green spaces and on the other hand requires those groups to accept certain criteria of public benefit in the way they work: 'Applicants will need to ensure that projects are inclusive, meet local needs and have local support. Specifically the proposed project should:

- meet the needs of the whole community by engaging a range of people and consulting on the needs of all users;

- demonstrate good practice in community and partnership based approaches to green space improvements;

- be deliverable and have plans for the long-term care of the site;

- relate to community, green space or other relevant local strategies.' (p102)

Assuming that these criteria are applied with a fairly light touch, this model could be regarded as amounting to a hybrid form of public service by the community sector, something between the autonomous public service provided by wholly self-governing community initiatives and the contracting out of regulated services to professionally organised bodies in the voluntary sector. We will return to these crucial distinctions in chapter four.

The Deputy Prime Minister's report on sustainable communities was published in February 2003[52]. The language of sustainable development originally came into public policy via the environmentalist movement and in particular the United Nations Rio summit of 1992. One of the most successful recommendations of that summit was the spreading of environmentalist action at local level by means of what came to be known as Local Agenda 21 schemes. Community involvement was axiomatic in Local Agenda 21, not only to drive environmental actions but as a factor in sustainability in itself. Environmentalist debate has not always been clear about the difference between enlisting communities to support the environment and the question of what makes communities themselves sustainable. It is good to see a major initiative in which the latter issue takes centre stage. But how does this relate to government policy on sustainable development as a whole?

[51] www.urban.odpm.gov.uk

[52] ODPM (2003), *Sustainable communities: Building for the Future.* London: ODPM (February).

In the government's sustainable development indicators published in 1999[53] there was a substantial section entitled *Building sustainable communities*. There were 150 indicators in the entire document, and 27 in this section. 25 of these were about economic performance, health, travel, access to services, access to culture and sport, housing, planning and design, local environment and crime. The last two, headed 'Involving everyone' were 'voluntary activity to promote social inclusion and cohesion' and 'help build a sense of community by encouraging and supporting all forms of community involvement'. Neither of these were amongst the 14 headline indicators which would primarily guide policy on sustainability, though they have been used in the *Quality of Life Counts*.[54]

The residual appearance of the community involvement aspect in a policy supposedly 'putting people at the centre', and continuing in its subsequent stages[55], was in striking contrast to the ethos of participation in the Agenda 21 movement. A ten year retrospect on Agenda 21[56] suggests a substantial volume of low-profile achievement by communities: 'Community groups are leading the way in taking practical action for sustainable development ... The community sector has a massive impact. Community-based recycling groups now serve one in six UK homes. Community organisations refurbish and distribute over a million items of funiture to low income groups each year. Over 11,000 groups take part in wildlife conservation ... Community groups manage farmers' markets, promote local and organic food, work to fight pollution and to lobby government ... 10 million passenger journeys per year are made using community transport schemes.'

However it is not always easy to make the transition from direct local good works to participation in local decision-making. Young estimates[57] that whilst virtually all local authorities in the UK eventually fulfilled the government's commitment to Local Agenda 21, only 50 to 60 councils in England achieved a thoroughgoing approach. Participation was sometimes neutralised where local councils had commitments to major building or economic programmes which they did not want compromised, or where councils took the view that participation meant a limited form of consultation. Large scale decisions on issues of planning and transport were mostly out of the reach of local residents' influence.

The Agenda 21 track record is of more than passing significance for the prospects for general community involvement. Agenda 21 has been arguably one of the most successful government and local government-endorsed mechanisms of local involvement and is often cited as a source of community experience and networks for the formation of LSPs. But local Agenda 21, which has not always been powerful across local government, may lose ground in being subsumed into community strategies: 'LA21 co-ordinators have usually

[53] DETR (1999) *A Better Quality of Life. A Strategy for Sustainable Development for the United Kingdom.* London: DETR (May).

[54] See www.sustainable-development.gov.uk/indicators/index.htm

[55] DEFRA (2003) *Achieving a Better Quality of Life. Review of Progress Towards Sustainable Development.* London: Department for Environment, Food and Rural Affairs (February). For comparison, a set of sustainability indicators produced for West Devon by a community-based organisation, also supported by DEFRA, combines some of the national indicators with other socio-economic ones and has as its first indicator 'Level of personal involvement in community groups': Savage, Jane and Emmett, Jeanette (2003) *Sustainability Indicators Report 2003.* Tavistock: West Devon Environmerntal Network.

[56] Church, Chris (2002) *The Quiet Revolution.* Birmingham: Shell Better Britain Campaign, p2.

[57] Young, Stephen (2000) 'Participation strategies and environmental politics' in Jerry Stoker, Ed., *The New Politics of British Local Governance*, London: Macmillan.

been placed either within environmental health or planning departments within their local authority … (and) have found it difficult to make the right links with mainstream economic and social programmes … (There are) striking similarities between LA21 and community strategies… Guidance encourages local authorities to make use of LA21 (in developing community strategies)… but many councils are abandoning LA21 and setting up new structures … Much of the knowledge and experience gained in the ten years since LA21 was launched is failing to be transferred.'[58]

The Lucas report looked at detailed case studies in Middlesbrough, Southampton, East Riding of Yorkshire, Renfrewshire, Bolton, Derry, Southwark and Caerphilly. Five key themes emerged from interviews with local people and front-line workers:

- local projects need to have community ownership to be successful in the long term;

- tokenistic community involvement can be damaging … by not following through with action;

- community-led projects often end up being run by one or several key local people who can get burnt out;

- it is difficult to measure the outputs of local projects against the traditional indicators set by funders, which inadequately describe the real worth of such initiatives.

- LA21 is generally not recognised as a label by communities but they have an inherent understanding of the need to take a sustainable development or joined up approach to regeneration (p51).

Church and Elster studied 17 local community-based projects with sustainable development aims, carrying out a variety of social, environmental and economic activities.[59] Although the individual impacts were often by their nature small-scale, the cumulative impact of such projects across the country was estimated to be considerable. But the potential impact and influence of the projects was often limited by their weak position in relation to other partners: 'Partnership implies a roughly equal relationship, yet most do not have that standing … Smaller projects are frequently in a client relationship … to a local authority or other large body. As projects develop so they acquire a degree of self-reliance … (then) a more balanced approach emerges: they can develop work in co-operation while maintaining their own identity (but) partnership in the sense of equality of stature and a formalised working agreement seemed to be the exception rather than the rule' (Summary, p3).

The 2003 Sustainable Communities plan is not only, as one might imagine from press reports, about the siting of new settlements. It reinforces and advances the government's policy discourse on local development in general. It refreshes some of the principles of the Urban White Paper, and it 'promotes' community involvement to a prominent place in the concept. 'What makes a sustainable community?' is answered by twelve factors, the

---

[58] Lucas, Karen, Ross, Andrew and Fuller, Sara (2002), *There's more than one way to skin a cat – From Local Agenda 21 to Community Planning and Beyond.* London: University of Westminster, Centre for Sustainable Development (October), p6-7.

[59] Church, Chris and Elster, Jake (2002) *Thinking Locally, Acting Nationally: Lessons for Policy from Local Action on Sustainable Development.* York: York Publishing Services for thre Joseph Rowntree Foundation, and London: Community Development Foundation.

third of which is 'effective engagement and participation by local people, groups and businesses, especially in the planning, design and long term stewardship of their community, and an active voluntary and community sector' (Overview, p2). This is backed up later in the list by 'vibrant local culture' and 'a sense of place'. The other elements are economy, leadership, environment, amenities, transport, buildings, homes, public services and regional, national and international links.

However, apart from the community enablers scheme introduced in *Living Places*, there are few clear footholds for the community involvement commitment in the accompanying budget structure. The financial implications of supporting community involvement are perhaps expected to be mainly covered by existing programmes such as Neighbourhood Renewal and New Deal for Communities but the lack of specific objectives for this major plank of the concept is disturbing.

There are other categories of spending from which community participation might conceivably benefit but in the overall conception the community involvement theme appears to have the 'high rhetoric, low specifics' status which is familiar in the 'disappearing community' syndrome.

There is clearly a lot more development of detail to be done under this plan and it is to be hoped that community involvement will be properly structured into such features as the 'Regional Centres of Excellence which will bring together key agencies and learning providers to drive forward the skills and knowledge agenda for everyone involved in creating sustainable communities'.

However, in so far as this plan is about what its title proclaims, it must be said that there is a worrying gap in provision for making the networks and organisations of the community itself sustainable. Much of the rationale for the planned increase in house-building is to do with the trend for increasing numbers of single-person households (currently believed to be 30% and rising) which suggests a clear need for better neighbourhood networks and activities. And given the emphatic commitment elsewhere that 'effective public engagement should be at the heart of development plans' (see section on planning, below), this gap is only thrown into relief by an allocation 'to help communities become more involved in the planning process'of £4m over three years, out of a total budget of £22bn.

2.9 Community involvement in specific spheres

The community involvement ethos is an aspect of modernisation in each of the main services. How it applies in each service is being worked out in detail within the culture of that service. Before concluding this review of policy landmarks it is apt to fill out the picture of this expanding field by glancing at ways in which community involvement has become more prominent within specific social issue areas in parallel with its growth in the strategic areas outlined above. We cannot give a comprehensive review, three examples illustrate the range.

2.9.1 BLACK AND MINORITY ETHNIC COMMUNITIES

The 1997 edition of *Involving Communities in Urban and Rural Regeneration* included new sections on involving ethnic minorities, faith communities and young people. The section on involving ethnic minorities[60] highlights the need to address specifically these communities and suggests how the general advice on techniques of consultation and involvement may need to be adapted in order to reach members of these communities. Each identifiable ethnic group should itself be consulted about the way in which it is appropriate for that group to be involved. 'Show you have the support of accepted leaders but are not in their pocket'. The guidance points to questions needing special attention, such as language, gender, sensitivity to culture, avoidance of tokenism, possible conflicts that may arise, and the 'go-between' role that children sometimes find themselves performing where they speak English better than their parents.

Race equality is tackled in a more head-on way in the 'Race equality guidance' produced for New Deal for Communities projects two years later[61]. Here the issue was not merely involvement but overcoming racism and disadvantage. Reflecting the Stephen Lawrence inquiry which had just taken place[62], the guidance urged NDC projects to address both overt and institutional racism and argued that improvements in race equality benefit not just those immediately affected but the locality as a whole: 'Diversity is an advantage'. It then showed, with mini-case studies, how equality can be promoted in jobs, education, health and overcoming crime.

The function of the black voluntary sector as a vital channel for the participation of black and minority ethnic (BME) communities in regeneration was stressed by a study carried out for a major voluntary-sector led regeneration partnership[63]. This argued that even where funders recognised the needs of black communities, these communities could not properly participate in the regeneration agenda if the black voluntary sector was marginalised in relation to the mainstream voluntary sector. 'The black voluntary sector today is a vibrant sector and has an enormous potential to contribute to regeneration. However... it continues to be marginalised... and is small in terms of financial resources' (p8). Drawing on voluntary sector surveys in Bolton and Bury, West Midlands and London, the report judged that the sector was strong in the sense of being close to and trusted by its grassroots members but weak in the kind of infrastructure and bureaucracy necessary to participate in regeneration partnerships.

It had long been suspected that surveys of volunteering did not fully capture the informal volunteering that takes place in BME communities because the people doing it rarely describe it as volunteering. A study in South West England, arising from the Active Community Unit's 'Twinning' project between BME and 'mainstream' organisations[64] argued that in BME communities there is extensive mutual aid and reliance but that most

---

[60] DETR (1997) *Involving Communities in Urban and Rural Regeneration*. London: ODPM. Revised edition. Pp 132ff.

[61] DETR (1999), *New Deal for Communities, Race Equality Guidance*. London: ODPM.

[62] Macpherson, W. (1999) *The Stephen Lawrence Inquiry*. London: HMSO.

[63] Zahno, Kamila and KENTE (1997), *Working with the Black voluntary sector, Good practice guide*. London: Pan London Community Regeneration Consortium (c/o British Associaton of Settlements).

[64] Kamat, Anita (2001), *Room for Growth, Patterns and Potential in Black and Minority Ethnic Volunteering*. Bristol: Black Development Agency and London: Community Development Foundation.

of the active people would be surprised to hear it called volunteering. The study also threw light on the recent 'community cohesion' debate[65] about the degree of separation of communities and the potential for 'cross-cultural' volunteering. Interviews with a small sample of mainly younger volunteers from BME communities revealed that about a third volunteered in BME organisations, and had made a specific decision to do so, a third in 'mainstream' (white-led) organisations, about a quarter in both, and a handful specifically in multicultural organisations. Only 18% had specifically chosen to volunteer within their own community. White-led organisations were generally keen to attract more diverse volunteers but frequently didn't know how to put these opportunities across successfully to BME communities; and some BME organisations had difficulty recruiting or retaining volunteers because they were less well resourced and sometimes lacked specific structures and practices for recruiting, training and retaining volunteers.

New dialogue on community cohesion during 2002-03 has thrown into relief the question of how respect for the needs of distinct ethnic communities should be balanced by fostering positive relationships between different ethnic communities. Guidance on community cohesion[66] sought to affirm both the valuing of diversity and the development of positive relationships between people from different backgrounds in the workplace, in schools and in neighbourhoods. At the same time, government recognises that equality cannot be achieved without supporting networks of BME organisations alongside mainstream networks, and provides such support at regional level.

2.9.2 PLANNING

Reforms of the planning system were heralded in a Green Paper in December 2001[67] which judged that the current plans system often failed to effectively engage the community or to integrate planning with other local strategies. The reforms aimed to deliver housing, economic development, transport and rural regeneration objectives in a sustainable way. Key principles include creating and sustaining mixed and inclusive communities, and enabling local communities to be involved 'much more positively than before' in planning decisions.[68]

The aim of the reforms is not merely to achieve better decisions, 'adding value to communities through better design', but decisions which elicit more widespread understanding and consent because there has been more widespread involvement in reaching them. 'We want a culture which promotes planning as a positive tool: a culture which grasps the opportunities to improve the experience of planning for those affected by its decisions, whether businesses, community groups, individual members of the community or planning professionals'.[69]

[65] Home Office (2001), *Building Cohesive Communities*. Ministerial group on public order and community cohesion (Denham report). London: Home Office; and Home Office (2001) *Community Cohesion, Report of the Independent Review Team* (Cantle report). London: Home Office.

[66] Local Government Association, ODPM, Home Office and CRE (2002) *Guidance on Community Cohesion*. London: LGA

[67] ODPM (2001), *Planning: Delivering a Fundamental Change* (Green paper). London: ODPM (December).

[68] ODPM (2002) *Sustainable communities: delivering through planning*. Planning policy statement. London: ODPM (July), para 3.

[69] Ibid para 6.

The key planning tool is to be a **Local Development Framework** prepared by the unitary or district planning authority, consisting of a core strategy, a proposal section and area action plans for key areas of change or conservation. The core strategy is required to include a statement of community involvement setting out benchmarks for community participation in the preparation of the framework and in significant planning applications.[70]

In addition, the policy intends to make the process for handling planning applications more transparent, ensure that people have cheap and easy access to documents, and to help individuals and community groups to develop planning advocacy skills and have better access to quality training and planning advisory services.[71]

The Green Paper was generally welcomed for its proposals to forge a stronger link between local development plans and the Community Strategies. 'The Local Development Framework should be a key component of the delivery plan (of the Community Strategy), setting out the spatial aspects of the local authority's policies...

It is a fundamental principle of our proposals that effective public engagement should be at the heart of development plans... we want to empower local people to feel that they can participate in a system that is really interested in their views. We want to change the culture of planning from one of objecting to one of constructive participation'.[72]

The obligatory statement of community involvement should set out:

- the arrangements and standards to be achieved in involving the community in the continuing review of all parts of the Local Development Framework;

- the standard of good practice to be achieved in engaging those with an interest in proposed development;

- clear guidelines enabling the community to know with confidence when and how it will be consulted, by the developer at pre-application stage and the LPS in relation to planning applications; and

- a benchmark for applicants for planning permission about what is expected of them.

(para 31).

ODPM is carrying out research on how the relationship between Local Development Frameworks and Local Strategic Partnerships would work best.

[70] Ibid paras 33-36.

[71] Ibid paras 61-63.

[72] ODPM (2002), *Making the System Work Better – Planning at Regional and Local Levels*. London: ODPM, paras 22-30.

2.9.3   HEALTH

Reforms in the health system mirror the principles applied in local government modernisation. The NHS Plan of July 2000[73] identified 'over-centralisation and disempowered patients' as one of the problems in the system. Whilst announcing massive new investment in the NHS ('The March 2000 budget settlement means that the NHS will grow by one half in cash terms and one third in real terms in just five years') the Plan also imposed a centrally-directed form of decentralisation similar to that being applied to local authorities through Comprehensive Performance Assessment as announced in the *Strong Local Leadership* White Paper.[74] A new system of 'earned autonomy' would devolve power from the government to the local health service as modernisation proceeded. The DoH would set national standards, matched by regular inspection of all local health bodies by an independent inspectorate, the Commission for Health Improvement. Local NHS organisations that performed well for patients would get more freedom to run their own affairs. But the government would intervene more rapidly in those parts of the NHS that failed their patients.

The Plan asserted that there was 'a new national alliance behind a reformed, patient-centred NHS. These are the most fundamental and far-reaching reforms the NHS has seen since 1948 … Over the next few years the NHS will be modernised from top to toe'. Social services and the NHS would be required to pool resources. There would be new Care Trusts to commission health and social care in a single organisation. This would help prevent patients, particularly old people, 'falling into the cracks between the two services or being left in hospital when they could be safely in their own home'.

'For the first time patients will have a real say in the NHS. They will have new powers and more influence over the way the NHS works … (including) patients' surveys and forums to help services become more patient-centred'; and for the first time there would be national inequalities targets to show whether primary care was being increased and improved in deprived areas.

This was followed up by the establishment in late 2002 of the Commission for Patient and Public Involvement in Health, whose job is 'to empower the public and patients so that they have a real say in decisions about service provision that affects them'[75]. The Commission will set and monitor quality standards for patients' forums and independent complaints advocacy services (ICAS), and produce training materials and guidance for patients' forums. It will also advise the Secretary of State for Health, and other bodies, on the arrangements for public involvement in the health service, and will conduct national reviews from a patients' and carers' perspective. Locally, staff supporting Primary Care Trust Patients' Forums will be responsible for finding out from local communities issues of concern relating to the quality and availability of services in their local area, ensuring that those views are represented to the PCT or NHS trust and enabling the public to get involved in the decision-making process.

The changes in the sphere of health will also have impacts on other issues, for example employment, as the NHS is one of the largest employers in Europe, let alone the UK.

---

[73] Department of Health (2000) *The NHS Plan,* London: DoH (July), and *The NHS Plan, A Summary.* Also at: www.nhs.uk/nationalplan/summary.htm

[74] DTLR (2001), *Strong Local Leadership, Quality Public Services.* London: ODPM.

[75] Department of Health (2002), *Commission for Patient and Public Involvement in Health (Functions) Regulations, Consultation Document,* London: Department of Health (September) [www.doh.gov.uk/cppihconsultation].

CHAPTER 3

What enables people to get involved or stops them from doing so?

3.1 The gap between guidance and analysis

What is the relationship between policy guidance on community involvement (reviewed in chapter two), the condition of urban communities themselves and the capacity of these communities to become involved?

The guidance literature, which, as we have seen, now amounts to a considerable library, has a general concern with deprivation but does not occupy itself much with the specific conditions of different communities. It mostly takes the community as a given, an 'untapped pool' of additional resources, and constructs its position on the basis of how authorities and partnerships ought to conduct themselves towards it.

The literature on urban development, conversely, is concerned with the condition of urban populations, the changing experience of cities over the last generation and the impact of social and economic change. Apart from a small number of studies, however, it does not examine how this affects the capacity of local populations to feel and act as communities, to sustain an effective community and voluntary sector and fulfil the opportunities provided by regeneration schemes and the new governance policies.

This chapter draws on a number of studies which do connect with both sides of the equation to suggest some of the factors in community life 'itself' which promote or impede community involvement and show some of its effects and some of the obstacles that stand in its way.

3.2 Towns and cities under the microscope

A broad array of comparative information on how urban areas across England have been coping with economic change and striving to move from selective regeneration to a general renaissance is provided by a partnership of 24 towns and cities led by the Urban Policy Unit of the Office of the Deputy Prime Minister. *Towns and Cities: Partners in Urban Renaissance* consisted of a programme of visits, studies and workshops between Oct 2001 and Oct 2002, facilitated by URBED[76]. The reports show that cities hard hit by industrial decline, mainly in the north, are slowly recovering but still have a long way to go: 'Major urban areas are not achieving their full potential despite positive trends across a

---

[76] URBED (Urban and Economic Development group) (2002), *Towns and Cities, Partners in Urban Renaissance. Project Report*, London: ODPM (October/ November). (Accompanying reports in the series are: *Partner Profiles; Case Studies; Workshops Report; Breaking Down the Barriers Report.*

number of indicators. Core cities[77] however are getting better. Loss of population seems to be slowing down, they have become centres for government and services such as law and accountancy, and they have benefited from the growth of their universities'[78]. Community involvement is identified as a key factor in recovery: 'The first dimension or precondition for urban renaissance is the participation of local residents and businesses in planning and delivery. Community engagement cuts across all steps in the process, and it goes beyond conventional consultation… The foundations for successful urban renaissance lie in making people feel they have some control over their lives, and some influence over what happens in their neighbourhood.'[79]

However, despite a number of examples of key roles played by community organisations and individual activists, 'community engagement is still in its infancy in most places'[80]. Workshops held with adults and young people found that people had strong views on what should happen to their cities or neighbourhoods but felt they were not being listened to. 'We must face up to a deep-rooted cynicism about the political process, combined with a babble of communications that are not getting through'[81].

Recommendations to overcome this, reflecting extant guidance literature, crystallise a number of good practice principles and mechanisms[82]:

- Area committees with budgets.

- Surveys and focus groups.

- Action planning using various techniques to secure involvement.

- Forums that meet periodically.

- Development Trusts that enable communities to acquire and manage assets.

- Community arts to raise aspirations and build capacity and confidence.

- Involvement of 'live wires' or community activists.

- Resources for capacity building.

- Special initiatives to involve young people.

All these are provided for in current policy and are being vigorously pursued in a number of areas, but it is too early to judge success on the combination of their effects.

[77] Birmingham, Bristol, Leeds, Liverpool, Manchester, Newcastle, Nottingham and Sheffield were designated 'core cities' on the basis of their distinctive role in regional and national economy – Ibid p42.

[78] Ibid p53.

[79] Ibid p89.

[80] Ibid p56.

[81] Ibid p89.

[82] Ibid p91.

Nash and Christie[83] suggest that in addition to policies devised specifically to stimulate community involvement, all policies affecting localities should be 'community proofed': 'We propose ... a community-proofing tool as a form of guidance for the design stage of national, regional and local policies ... to alert policy makers to the potential for improving local community relationships (and) to highlight the risks of inadvertently damaging local social capital and community cohesion ... It could be applied in such contexts as regeneration ... the development of faith-based schools ... proposals for new facilities ... development planning and ... design of new housing developments'.

Three types of test are put forward: firstly to ascertain whether the proposal would support or undermine a rich variety of social ties; secondly to ascertain whether the proposal would support or undermine trust and civility; and thirdly to ascertain whether the proposal would support or undermine local pride and identity. Questions to test these factors would cover whether the proposal would:

- erode or enhance local spaces and places for congregation and interaction;

- discourage or encourage the development of community action networks;

- erect or reduce physical barriers to interaction between different local social groups;

- create or reduce social and cultural monocultures;

- foster or allay resentment and conflict between communities;

- encourage or discourage crime and antisocial behaviour;

- undermine or enhance the quality of the streetscape;

- destroy or protect local landmarks positively associated with the community;

- encourage or discourage stigmatisation of the area;

- reduce or increase the quality of the local built and green environment.

One would want to add similar proofing regarding whether a proposal would enhance or diminish the effectiveness of the local community and voluntary sector.

3.3 Disadvantage impedes participation

The trauma undergone by the formerly heavily industrialised cities of northern and Midland Britain, and some smaller areas in the south, is well known, but what effect have the economic changes of the last generation had on community life?

[83] Nash, Victoria and Christie, Ian (2003) *Making Sense of Community*, London: Institute for Public Policy Research (IPPR) (February), pp 82-84.

Richardson and Mumford[84] attribute social breakdown in four areas they studied to these historic factors:

- large-scale building of public housing on the back of slum clearance, accompanied by allocations policies which came to exclude all but the most needy, created stigmatised areas of last resort;

- industrial restructuring from the early 1970s onwards decimated the manual jobs that so many of the inner city residents relied on, and pushed out the more skilled and ambitious;

- suburbanisation and increasing ease of owner-occupation encouraged the better-off to flee from cities, while the release of greenfield land outside cities created a ready supply of relatively cheap housing;

- city-wide depopulation resulted in extremely high turnover and rate of exodus from the poorest areas.

Mooney and Danson paint a picture of post-industrial Glasgow and the surrounding area in the mid 90s as a 'dual city', one section of the population able to benefit from the 'new economy' of recovery, the other – larger – section depleted and excluded. '44% of manufacturing and 5% of service jobs disappeared from the city between 1981 to 1991 … 12% of the regional population live in the areas of severe deprivation … (where) unemployment was at least 27% … Between 1981-91 the peripheral estates lost 30% of their population and the rural areas as a whole lost 20% … Lone parents headed over 35% of households, and 52% of the non-elderly population were limited by long-term illnesses'[85]. The large expansion in the new service sector in the 1980s (banking, finance, personal services, tourism and administration), all promoted as key elements of the post-industrial city and as compensation for the loss of skilled manufacturing employment, overwhelmingly benefited commuters outside the city. Nearly half of all jobs were now taken by residents in the dormitory suburbs, satellite towns and other regions.

Such a haemorrhage of jobs and people is bound to damage community capacity. Yet community involvement is naturally particularly sought in disadvantaged areas. The Home Office Active Citizenship survey[86] shows that there is less volunteering and a less dense community and voluntary sector profile in the deprived areas than in well-off areas. Community activity and involvement is not an attribute of disadvantage but another one of the social goods which disadvantaged areas lack. (A good deal of disadvantage is of course spread less visibly in advantaged areas).

The association of disadvantage with a lower level of community involvement is borne out by the annual survey of sources of information on poverty that has been published by the Joseph Rowntree Foundation for the past five years. These include, amongst some fifty sources on material aspects of poverty, one on 'civic participation' and one on 'satisfaction

84 Richardson, Liz and Mumford, Katherine (2002), 'Community, neighbourhood and social infrastructure' in John Hills and Julian Le Grand, *Understanding Social Exclusion*, Oxford: OUP, p206-7.

85 Mooney, G and Danson, M. (1997) 'Beyond 'Culture City': Glasgow as a 'Dual City''in Jewson, N and MacGregor, S., *Transforming Cities*. London: Routledge (p82-3).

86 Op cit.

with local area'.[87] According to these reviews, in 2000-01 there were 13 million people living in relatively low income households, a fall of one million (7%) since 1996-7. This was still double the figure of 20 years before. People were asked whether they participated in trade unions, professional associations, parents' associations, pensioner groups, community and tenant groups, women's groups, religious groups, sports and social groups and political parties. There is a clear pattern showing some correlation between wealth and participation. 57% of the richest fifth, 45% of the middle three fifths and 37% of the poorest fifth participate. However, at least 40% in all categories do not participate.

If poverty impedes participation, concentrations of poverty in particular neighbourhoods magnify the difficulty. But a Joseph Rowntree Foundation study looking at poverty and home ownership[88] finds that whilst overall:

- 25% of the adult population of the UK are living in poverty;

- 2% are rising from poverty;

- 12% are at risk of poverty; and

- 61% do not live in poverty.

Poverty is by no means confined to those living in social housing. 41% of those living in poverty live in social housing, 9% are in the private rented sector and 50% are owner-occupiers. Factors associated with poverty amongst owner-occupiers are worklessness, single parenthood, ethnic minority background, divorce, separation and living in the Midlands or Wales. The report suggests that area-based initiatives aimed at overcoming poverty are missing a large part of their target by focusing mostly on concentrations of social housing.

3.4 Stimulating involvement

Whether there has yet been a significant increase of involvement of communities as a result of recent policies is not certain. Some observers are tentatively positive: 'Looking across British government in the 1990s, it is not possible to draw clear conclusions about the impact of participatory experiments. Some writers take an optimistic view ... others remain critical about the impact. It is possible to find examples to confirm both ... but the variety of innovatory approaches and the scale on which they are being adopted seem more substantial than at any time since the 1969 Skeffington report.'[89]

---

[87] Rahman, Mohibur and others (2001), *Monitoring Poverty and Social Exclusion 2001.* York: Joseph Rowntree Foundation; Palmer, Guy and others (2002), *Monitoring Poverty and Social Exclusion 2002,* York: Joseph Rowntree Foundation.

[88] Burrows, Roger (2003) Poverty and Home Ownership in Contemporary Britain. Abingdon: The Policy Press (January).

[89] Stephen Young (2000), 'Participation strategies and environmental politics' in Jerry Stoker, Ed., *The New Politics of British Local Governance,* Macmillan.

The multiplication of regeneration partnerships, area forums or neighbourhood initiatives of one kind or another must mean that one could show an increase in the number of individuals drawn into this process. The picture is somewhat obscured however by the tendency in much of the community involvement literature to use community indiscriminately to mean community representatives, community groups or local residents as a whole. It is difficult to get a sense of the proportions of local people who might be involved. One evaluation document speaks of a bus project for teenagers 'acquired, decorated and driven by the community'. Rare studies that make clear distinctions between active participants, representatives and the local population as a whole may reveal large gaps between an involved minority and uninvolved majority. In a study in Merseyside, officials regarded 'the community' as having a good deal of influence on the huge regeneration scheme whilst three quarters of residents did not know the scheme existed[90].

Tenant Management Organisations, operating since 1993 under the statutory right to manage for council tenants, with background support and promotion from ODPM, have a good record of involvement and can also show some advantages over traditional service delivery in this area. Research commissioned by ODPM[91] shows that TMOs make an effective contribution to developing more sustainable communities, despite many operating on estates with histories of disadvantage. Many TMOs are as good as the best local authorities in terms of getting repairs done and 77% of tenants were satisfied with TMO management compared with 67% satisfied with council management.

Environmentalist groups received a particular boost from Local Agenda 21: 'LA21 in the UK has spawned a huge number of local initiatives over the last ten years … It is estimated that there are literally thousands of projects, programmes and policy initiatives running in the UK today that have their base in LA21'.[92] However, many LA21 programmes have struggled to recruit individuals unused or unwilling to engage in formal political processes: 'Black and minority ethnic and deprived and excluded communities are under-represented and both the youth and the older section of the population have been passed over.'

If environmentalist groups find it hard to involve disadvantaged people, that may be because they do not sufficiently connect with the problems of the immediate urban environment which is undoubtedly a major preoccupation for people who live in distressed neighbourhoods. In a New Deal for Communities estate on the outskirts of Coventry, residents described the constant fear of having their homes and cars broken into, verbal abuse on the streets, and the common public spaces being filled with burnt-out cars[93]. Despite having had major regeneration investment for 15 years the area had not lost its stigma, high unemployment and low educational attainment. Crime and anti-social behaviour had contributed to a recent dramatic rise in voids and turnover which improvements in the early 1990s had reduced. A tenants' leader said that anti-social behaviour was difficult to deal with because tenants were frightened to report it.

[90] Paul Kyprianou (1999), *Community Participation and Partnership, A Review of Participation in the Liverpool Objective One Partnerships.* Liverpool: Liverpool Euro Community Network.

[91] ODPM (2002) *The Importance of Tenant Management Organisations in Developing Sustainable Communities.* London: ODPM, November (summary at: www.housing.odpm.gov.uk/signpost/iss014/07.htm)

[92] Lucas, Karen, Ross, Andrew and Fuller, Sara (2002), *There's more than one way to skin a cat – From Local Agenda 21 to Community Planning and Beyond.* London: University of Westminster, Centre for Sustainable Development (October), p5-6.

[93] Audrey Gillan, 'Where the law abiding live in fear'. The Guardian, Monday November 11, 2002.

Nevertheless, community involvement held out hope of improvement. Various projects including a neighbourhood warden scheme were in the pipeline. 'Such schemes have been successful on Castle Vale estate in nearby Birmingham ... Heralded as a success story for neighbourhood regeneration, it has a waiting list for its houses.' This seems to have been achieved by a form of approved vigilantism. Some tenants had walkie talkies and patrolled the area. CCTV cameras were being installed. Warning notices about anti-social behaviour were served on a number of families. Some reformed their ways. Five were taken to court and eventually evicted. The housing manager said 'Residents have taken it into their own hands and it is working'.

Brian Robson believes that despite the ravages of poverty, most deprived areas still have potential for involvement: 'Even in the most deprived communities there are considerable social strengths on which policy could build. Surveys consistently show that high proportions of residents in deprived areas value the quality of people in their neighbourhoods and argue that the problems of crime, dereliction and social disruption are caused by a small minority. This suggests that almost all deprived communities retain elements of their traditionally strong community structures. Much of this is maintained by women, particularly the middle aged and elderly'[94].

Richardson and Mumford[95] suggest that only a combination of determined community action and determined public policy can rebuild a deteriorating locality: 'The strong signals of neglect and unpopularity sent out by poor physical conditions, poor local economy and boarded up homes contributed to the remaining population feeling demoralised and isolated ... All aspects of social infrastructure were threatened: facilities, services and social organisation. The threat could not be lifted by community action alone. But the formal services – such as police, housing, education – could not do it on their own either'.

However, in order to achieve this, a number of residents had to work strenuously for many years, and of course at their own expense, to establish and maintain a number of key organisations and networks amongst the local community. So far from being an 'untapped pool' which could simply be accessed by public initiatives, the residents' efforts were themselves a conscious major input with its own opportunity costs in terms of their personal life and household strategies.

Local participation also has many-sided benefits in less extreme situations. Plymouth Community Partnership's 'Local social capital' project, which ran from 1998-2001[96], set up ward panels of local residents across the city to help disburse small grants for a wide variety of very local projects on such things as childcare, youth activities, facilities for the elderly, arts, transport for the visually impaired, carnivals, newsletters, parenting etc. 120 grants of up to £6,000 were made, totalling £600,000.

94 Robson, Brian (2000) 'Key challenges for the Urban White Paper', *Cityscape* (newsletter of the ESRC Cities competitiveness and cohesion programme). Liverpool: European Institute for Urban Affairs, Liverpool John Moore University (Autumn).

95 Richardson, Liz and Mumford, Katherine (2002), 'Community, neighbourhood and social infrastructure' in John Hills and Julian Le Grand, *Understanding Social Exclusion*, Oxford: OUP, p206-7.

96 Plymouth Community Partnership (2002), *Local Social Capital Pilot Project Final Evaluation Report*, Plymouth: Plymouth Community Partnership.

Of particular interest in terms of involvement was the effect on the 246 local residents who were voluntarily involved in the 19 ward-level committees making the grant decisions. 20 were interviewed about the effect on themselves of their participation in this process. Virtually all said that through this process they had made new friends, half said it had increased their confidence and over half that they had gained new skills. 17 of the twenty said they had a better awareness of what was going on in their area, 15 had developed a new interest and 13 said they felt less isolated. Nine felt more able to cope with their problems, five felt more competent in their employment and four felt more able to obtain employment (ibid, p24).

Overall, the evidence for the feasibility and effectiveness of community involvement at a small local level such as the neighbourhood or ward is more secure than at the LSP or local authority-wide level. A review of the evidence base for regeneration produced for ODPM in 1999-2000[97] found that 'area based initiatives have been successful in targeting benefits to the most disadvantaged households in deprived areas when they have specifically addressed the needs of groups of disadvantaged … and have set up tailor-made projects for each group … managed by resident community groups' (p4); but that at the level of local authority wide partnerships there are recurrent problems such as a sense of marginalisation on the part of the community and voluntary sectors and difficulties of sustaining a consistent response from representatives. Nevertheless, Lawless and his colleagues recognise that whilst 'the neighbourhood is the most appropriate area for fostering community identity, involvement and neighbourhood management', schemes limited to deprived neighbourhoods may take too little account of opportunities in other parts of a city and may not be able to address problems arising in slightly less deprived neighbourhoods.

3.5 Is the new governance working?

It is too early to assess whether the 'new governance' of community strategies and LSPs is making a wide difference to involvement. Local community groups not infrequently allege that local authorities and the other 'big players' implement their community involvement obligations in purely token and 'top-down' ways[98]. It is sometimes alleged that decisions have been 'stitched up' by the powerful players behind closed doors whilst communities or their representatives are in theory being involved[99]. Nor does the era of 'new governance' prevent councils from pulling the grants rug out from under the local community and voluntary sector when financial pressures loom.

A report for the Urban Summit of 2002 by Urban Forum and the Black Training and Enterprise Group judged that the structures for community participation and engagement in urban policy were bewildering for many would-be participants, despite the advent of LSPs[100]. 'In the absence of clear structures, decision-making processes and funding streams, the sector must engage with the myriad of structures through which these elements of

[97] Lawless, Paul et al (2000) *A Review of the Evidence Base for Regeneration Policy and Practice*, London: ODPM/ www.urban.odpm.gov.uk

[98] Not often documented but see for example *Response to West Devon Community Plan*, Okehampton Locality Group, August 2002.

[99] Eg Monbiot, George 'Breaking point – the smashing of Southampton' in *Captive State, The Corporate Takeover of Britain.* London: Macmillan, 2000.

[100] Mackie, Liz (2002), *Putting People at the Heart of the Urban Renaissance*. London: BTEG (Black Training and Enterprise Group) and Urban Forum (November).

urban policy are managed ... (These) create further layers of gatekeepers, with policy makers and funders at the top layer and VCS (voluntary and community sector) organisations and local communities at the bottom ... As policy and programme implementation work their way down these layers, funding decreases and bureaucracy multiplies. Despite the government's intention that LSPs will rationalise and co-ordinate activity at a local level, LSPs remain just one amongst many partnerships and structures which the sector must engage with. The sector's experience of LSPs to date is mixed but two common themes are emerging from a great number of difficult local experiences: (a) the VCS is the least well resourced and therefore the minority partner; (b) local authorities often use the power which their size and greater resources gives them to dominate the partnership'.

This is borne out by a Joseph Rowntree Foundation study of the governance needs of small community groups. Twenty groups and organisations were selected from such fields as refugees, community arts, disability, self-help, with an emphasis on new and emerging groups: 'Government policies of contracting-out, tackling social exclusion and promoting social entrepreneurship, intended to stimulate an increase in local activities, have added to confusion, because of their emphasis on different aspects of governance. Small community groups and organisations ... have been pulled in different directions'.[101]

Nevertheless, success stories are beginning to emerge. An example of an LSP with striking results even after only a year of operation can be found in the London Borough of Hillingdon. The year's programme of the LSP is driven by a borough-wide conference to which all community and voluntary organisations are invited. The 200 such organisations which attended the 2003 conference[102] included groups concerned with arts, ethnic identity, mental health, physical health, refugees, sports, local history, travellers, women, elderly, health service users, tenants and residents, neighbourhood improvement, town centre action, safety, allotments, small business, charitable fundraising, carer support, neighbourhood watch, lifelong education, citizens advice, playschemes, AIDS, needs of the blind, credit unions, narrowboats and dozens of other issues. They received reports back from the public services on action taken on priorities they had established the preceding year such as:

- improvements in street lighting;

- CCTV systems to monitor antisocial behaviour hotspots;

- a borough co-ordinator to organise methods to overcome antisocial behaviour;

- a mentoring system for young people who lack positive adult role models;

- help for vulnerable elderly people;

- information kiosks around the borough to provide help for people who are confronting domestic violence.

[101] Kumar, Sarabajaya and Nunan, Kevin (2002). *A Lighter Touch: An Evaluation of the Governance Project*, York: Joseph Rowntree Foundation and York Publishing Services.

[102] Hillingdon, London Borough of (2003) *Working Together for a Better Future: Hillingdon;s Community Conference.* London Borough of Hillingdon (February).

They then divided into neighbourhood groupings to consider new priorities, including a variety of forms of support for actions by the community and voluntary organisations themselves.

People's sense of involvement and willingness to become more involved clearly depends on a number of interacting factors. A community survey in Southwark by OPM[103] reveals illuminating patterns on such factors as a mixture of social capital and public involvement:

- whether people were attached to their neighbourhood;

- whether people get on with and trust other people living in their neighbourhood;

- how frequently people make use of each of the main services;

- what people feel needs improving in their neighbourhood;

- whether they feel that the various public services and voluntary organisations are interested in their views;

- whether they feel that the area is improving or declining.

Figures in a particularly disadvantaged area (Consort/Friary wards) were compared with those for the borough as a whole (much of which is disadvantaged relative to national averages). As much as a third of people in the borough as a whole, and nearly half the people in the especially disadvantaged area, felt that most of the people living in their area would like to move out. There were still substantial numbers however, who felt positive about their area and were willing to work to improve it.

Clearly, in order to commit to community involvement, people need to think they are going to stay in the locality for the foreseeable future. The huge turnover of residents in some blighted areas is both a reflection of intolerable conditions and a diminishment of the resources to improve them. In localities under stress many people undoubtedly face a fine emotional calculation between 'Should I get involved in trying to improve this place or try to get out and find somewhere better?'.

The quality of public services, which can vary even between adjacent neighbourhoods, is also affected by the community's capacity to monitor and access them. In the Southwark study, people in the disadvantaged area had less frequent contact with the health service, libraries, leisure centres and tenants' and residents' associations, voluntary organisations, councillors and the council itself than did people across the borough as a whole, though their need was clearly greater. They had more than average contact only with housing and social services.

[103] OPM (Office for Public Management) (1999), *Living in Consort and Friary Wards, A Community Survey*. London: OPM and Southwark Council.

When people were asked whether they felt that various services were interested in their views, only the health service was felt to be interested by more than half the respondents. Next most positive were libraries and leisure centres, tenants' and residents' associations and schools and nurseries. About a third of people felt that churches, voluntary and community organisations and the council as a whole were interested in their views, with social and housing services and local councillors below these. Again, on all counts except housing and social services, the interest perceived by people in the disadvantaged area was lower than for the borough as a whole.

It is increasingly recognised that greater community involvement will not come about unless there is a deep shift in the culture of public bodies and the style of professionals working in localities. The Neighbourhood Renewal Unit has articulated the aim of capacity building about community involvement within official institutions, as well as amongst residents, by proposing a 'learning curve' shared by residents, public service professionals, civil servants, local authority policy-makers, councillors and local organisations, with specific roles for the Government Offices of the Regions, Regional Development Agencies, Learning and Skills Councils, local authorities and LSPs.[104]

It is also notable, in the Southwark study, that the communities' 'own' organisations – tenants' associations, voluntary and community organisations – were not felt to be any more interested in people's views than some of the public services. This should help us to bear in mind that each community or voluntary organisation is identified with by a part, sometimes a small part, of the community, not by the community *en masse*.

Several other factors point to what might be called the psychology of community involvement, people in the disadvantaged area were less able or less motivated to put forward desired improvements than people across the borough as a whole even though their conditions and access to services were objectively worse. One gets an impression of a collective state of depression or withdrawal. Nevertheless, 45% of residents, both in the borough and the disadvantaged area, said they were willing to get involved in local improvement. This ever-hopeful response by a proportion of residents even in localities under stress represents the kind of energy which the government hopes to enlist through its policies on improving the physical condition of neighbourhoods.[105]

Further illumination of the psychology of community involvement comes from a US study[106]. This shows that, over and above the effects of poverty and disadvantage, people's capacity to participate in improving their conditions is significantly affected by their sense of order or disorder in their neighbourhood. Drawing on a large sample of 2,500 people across the state of Illinois, including highly urbanised Chicago on the one hand and a variety of rural areas on the other, they show that people's sense of powerlessness is affected over and above what would be expected from differences of poverty and advantage by the level of perceived order or disorder in the neighbourhood, in terms of crime, vandalism, noise, young people hanging around, abandoned buildings, neighbour conflicts, drug and alcohol use and general trust of others:

[104] ODPM (2002), *The Learning Curve*. London: ODPM, Neighbourhood Renewal Unit (October).

[105] ODPM (2002) *Living Places – Cleaner, Safer, Greener*. London: ODPM (October).

[106] Geis, Karlyn J. and Ross, Catherine E, (1998) 'A new look at urban alienation: the effect of neighbourhood disorder on perceived powerlessness', *Social Psychology Quarterly* (US), 61:3, 232-246.

'Neighbourhood disorder is an urban problem but the neighbourhood more than the city itself shapes people's sense of powerlessness ... Disorder has large independent effects on perceptions of powerlessness, over and above individual characteristics of race, education, income and employment ... But people who visit and talk with their neighbours and help each other out report significantly lower levels of powerlessness than do those without such ties' (p241-2).

This, like the Southwark study, suggests that the level of social capital is a determinant of participation. This proposition was examined through eight in-depth case-studies by Vivien Lowndes and others[107]. Four of the areas were broadly deprived, four were broadly well-off: East Hants; Middlesbrough (D); Sutton (London); Rotherham (D); Vale of the White Horse; Wellingborough (D); Merton (London); and Hull (D) were assessed both on population characteristics and levels of deprivation, on levels of community activity and on 'democratic innovation': local government attempts to improve democratic structures. They draw on the seminal work of Robert Putnam on social capital (see section on social capital in chapter four) but separate out social capital 'proper' from involvement in governance ('local political activity'), in order to see under what conditions they correlate. They looked for social capital in terms of:

- attachment to neighbourhood;

- trust in other people;

- how helpful people are perceived to be;

- how fair people are perceived to be; and

- membership of recreational organisations.

and involvement in governance in terms of:

- voting in local government election;

- contacting politicians or officials;

- signing a petition;

- boycotting products; and

- wearing a campaign badge.

They find that high levels of 'pure' social capital are an independent variable, affected but not wholly determined by levels of deprivation. But whether this social capital gets 'converted' into political participation is critically affected by how far the local polity is making corresponding efforts to 'seek out and welcome' community involvement: 'Social capital (has) a role in explaining different levels and styles of participation within areas of similar socio-economic status ... enhancing individuals' capacity to join together in

---

[107] Vivien Lowndes, Lawrence Pratchett and Gerry Stoker, *Social Capital and Political Participation: How do Local Institutions Constrain or Enable the Mobilisation of Social Capital?* Paper for Cambridge Social Capital Seminar 19 Nov 2002.

collective action to resolve common problems (or ensure that governments address such problems)' but 'whether social capital is mobilised as a resource for political engagement and democratic health depends on a variety of factors other than the level of social capital itself ... Particular local institutional arrangements – within civil society and the state – act either to constrain or enable the mobilisation of social capital as a resource for participation. Institutional rules both formal and informal ...influence the "conversion" of social capital' (pp1-3).

Differences were not explainable by socio-economic variables – high social capital was found in several relatively wealthy and deprived areas (p8). However, greater membership and density of local community and voluntary organisations appeared to be connected to level of political participation. They conclude: 'In some localities high levels of social capital may exist but not be invested in local politics. In other areas, lower levels of social capital may be more effectively mobilised ... we propose that there are three key institutional filters at work: political parties and leadership; public management; and the voluntary and community sectors' (p10).

Looking more closely at the community and voluntary sector, they judge that its structure and culture affects not just the absolute amount of social capital in a locality but also differences in the way in which social capital is mobilised. 'The voluntary and community sectors ... are also very different ... in their level of coordination, their approach to engagement and their relationship with the local authority ... In Hull relations between the local authority and the voluntary sector were often strained and confrontational, operating in an environment of mutual distrust ... Middlesbrough had a much more active and engaged voluntary sector that, while preserving its autonomy ... (had) a sense of common purpose across voluntary and community organisations and the local authority ... The history of different community and voluntary organisations and the history of interaction between them and the local state shapes expectations about which issues are open for participation, whose voice is likely to be most significant and the ways in which political differences can be resolved' (p15).

CHAPTER 4

Towards a unified approach to community involvement

4.1 A tectonic shift?

The time when it was necessary to argue that community involvement is a desirable aim has long since gone. The principle is writ large throughout current UK social policy. (This is not to say that that time could not come again.)

Community involvement has not yet, however, become securely embedded in practice. Partly this is simply attributable to lack of time. Between 1997 and 2003 there has been a broadening and deepening of policy on community involvement, proceeding rapidly through three phases:

(a) from a relatively limited number of regeneration schemes to a much larger number;

(b) from community involvement as an attribute of regeneration and a marginal aspect of other services to community involvement as a central aspect of virtually every public service;

(c) from a number of scattered partnerships to the principle of partnership as a main focus of local governance and service modernisation.

Partly, however, the gap between principle and implementation is caused by lack of clear objectives and strategy to bring it about.

It is too early to say how deep the changes will go and how effective the new governance mechanisms are. The underlying agenda is a massive experiment in shifting from a local representative democracy with a number of supplementary inputs towards a local democracy which is participative at a whole cascade of levels but still framed within a formal representative democratic structure.

4.2 Doubts

This 'new localism' has created a good deal of anxiety as well as excitement. It has been seen as endangering the power of central government to redistribute resources from richer to poorer areas and to impose equitable standards of services. It is sometimes regarded as threatening the role of elected councillors by giving powers to individuals designated as community representatives on an unclear basis. David Walker[108] warns against 'an unthinking embrace of what is being called the new localism. What if, along with local differences, go inequality, under-provision of vital services and capriciousness in their delivery ... We need a strong centre ... to combat inequality of local resources ... Should we celebrate the "diversity" of widespread poverty, huge inter-regional gaps in GDP per head and geographical concentrations of deprivation? ... How do these local and regional areas, freed from the iron hand of the centre, propose to raise their own resources from economic bases that may already be deprived by de-industrialisation and de-population? ... You cannot assume as some new localists do that community decisions will all be progressive and enlightened.'

Walker argues that in the 20th century progressive policies have largely flowed from central initiatives while local politics have more often than not been the homeground of reaction. 'Devolution is often, surreptitiously, an argument for shrinking the state and diminishing the capacity of government... Localists and advocates of regionalism need to beware of becoming stalking horses for smaller and weaker government.'

Marvin and Guy similarly warn against thinking that social problems can be solved locality by locality: 'In the new localist discourse the locality becomes viewed as some sort of container or black box which can be physically and socially shaped to deliver a more sustainable future... there is a powerful tendency to develop an inward looking approach... Individual, national and global relations... cannot be easily captured in the new localist agenda...Privatisation of water, sewage, energy and transport has created a new context...'[109]

These warnings should help us avoid the illusion that all problems can be solved at local level alone. However, even the most global approach cannot solve problems *without* special action at local level. The fact that conditions of advantage and disadvantage continue to differ acutely from one locality to another within the same country, region, city and even district clearly means that *some part* of the solution to these problems is inescapably local. Furthermore, any prospect of the majority of people feeling personally involved in the solutions demands varied meaningful action at local level. But there is no reason why local action has to be limited to a local *analysis*. On the contrary, the environmentalist slogan 'think global act local' holds as good as ever.

Nor does any of the guidance or policy we have reviewed seem to justify any notion that the empowering of communities makes the formal democratic system or its accountability for public services redundant. Community activity is essentially autonomous and therefore neither systematic nor democratically accountable (except to its self-selected members). It is therefore complementary to, not competitive with, the formal democratic system. Without that system it would have no authoritative decision-making arena in which to negotiate, seek influence and bid for support.

---

[108] Walker, David (2002a) *In Praise of Centralism: A Critique of the New Localism*. Catalyst Forum (October) and Walker, David (2002b) 'A lot of local difficulties', *Guardian Society*, Nov 18.

[109] Marvin, G. and Guy, M (1997) 'Creating myths rather than sustainability: the transition fallacies of the new localism', *Local Environment*, 2:3, pp 311-318.

4.3 Seven changing factors

The stream of guidance on community involvement in various programmes over the last ten, and particularly the last five, years furnishes many of the elements for a comprehensive approach to community involvement, working largely through programmes that are already in place. The general principles of the cumulative guidance have been broadly absorbed, and the policy focus has shifted to questions of how to disentangle the different purposes of involvement[110], how to implement it in practice and how to recognise and measure it[111]. But tracing the community involvement element through this short period of intensive development shows that different understandings and emphases rise and fall. Key points are found in a succession of documents which sometimes pass fairly quickly out of currency, leaving an uncertain residue.

This chapter reflects on some of the elements which are undergoing change. Seven issues are considered:

(i)   **Social capital.**

(ii) **Service provision.**

(iii) **Volunteering and public service.**

(iv) **The economic value of community activity.**

(v)   **Timescales for capacity building.**

(vi) **The position of community development.**

(vii) **The use of community indicators.**

The aim here is to advance some ideas about the role of these factors as potential components of a community involvement strategy.

4.4 Social capital: strengthening the intrinsic life of communities

The concept of social capital points to the importance of the intrinsic nature of community life. If we glance back at the triangle of aims we identified in the Urban White Paper[112] – governance, service delivery and social capital – it is the social capital angle, the intrinsic life of the community, which is the weakest in the policy stream.

---

[110] Ann MacFadyen, *Engaging with Communities: Disentangling Government Policy and Programmes that Impact on local NHS Organisations and Community Engagement*. London: Dept of Health, 2002 (Sept).

[111] Audit Commission, op. cit; Chanan, Gabriel (2002), *Measures of Community*. London: Active Community Unit (Home Office) and Community Development Foundation (July).

[112] DETR (2000), *Our Towns and Cities: The Future, Delivering and Urban Renaissance,* London: ODPM.

Much policy literature relies on an assumption that communities exist as entities to be mobilised or to have their capacity built for particular outcomes. However, there is also a recognition that many communities may be less stable and cohesive than they once were, for reasons both of poverty and prosperity. We need not subscribe to a romantic view of communities as ever having been wholly homogeneous and harmonious to recognise that in post-modern (or late modern) times there are many destabilising factors[113].

There is very much less literature on the effects of prosperity on community life than the effects of poverty, but the US policy analyst Robert Reich puts it like this:

'One of history's crowning achievements has been to give people a *choice* of community ... As with other aspects of your new life, you shop for the best community you can afford. Because exit is so easy and the benefits are so targeted, these new communities do not require nearly as much commitment as the old ones did, nor do they offer the same security to members who might need to depend on one another in a pinch. Sure, you develop friends in a childcare group, but you do not have to reveal as much about yourself along the way, you can end the friendship instantly, as can they ... The secession of middle and lower middle income families is also leading America back towards racially segregated neighbourhoods ... No one designed the system this way ... Many may in fact disapprove of the sorting that is occurring, to the extent that they are aware of it. But the sorting itself may reduce their awareness.'[114]

The ability of communities to contribute to policy outcomes depends on there being a certain critical mass of social capital. However, because social capital is fundamentally autonomous, its objectives cannot be prescribed by policy. 'Environments which favour networking ... are characterised by diversity, autonomy, voluntary choices, risk and turbulence ... Communication and co-operation tend to be based on personal relationships rather than formal rules ... Configurations cannot be predicted in advance ... In an uncertain, turbulent world, systems operate best within an intermediate zone somewhere between rigidity and randomness. This has become known [in complexity theory] as 'the edge of chaos".[115]

In putting a high value on community involvement, policies are trading on people's willingness to devote a considerable proportion of their free time, energy and sometimes money to voluntary collective local activity. Such policies are based either on the assumption that this is a natural public-spirited thing for people to do or that people consciously see it as a worthwhile investment from which they themselves also benefit.

What 'local governance' is implicitly saying to people is, in effect, 'You have much to gain by positively 're-embedding'[116] in your locality; by taking it seriously as a field of action and satisfaction. You may no longer depend on it economically or socially in the holistic, multi-layered way that people once used to but you are still highly affected by what happens in it. If you are not happy in it, you need not think only of moving; you have the

---

[113] Giddens, Anthony (1991), *The Consequences of Modernity*, Cambridge: Polity Press.

[114] Reich, Robert B. (2001) *The Future of Success, Work and Life in the New Economy*, London: William Heinemann.

[115] Gilchrist, Alison (2000): 'The well-connected community: networking to 'the edge of chaos". Oxford: Oxford University Press: *Community Development Journal*, 35:3, July, pp 265-269.

[116] Giddens, op cit.

opportunity to improve it and therefore influence major decisions which will shape its future. Large benefits can accrue to active participants over and above any altruistic or public-spirited interest in a better locality: extension of skills, networks, contacts, job-opportunities, and the satisfaction of feeling that you can influence what goes on around you.'

Whereas much of the guidance of the past five years sees conditions for involvement mainly in terms of how partnerships and authorities behave towards community representatives, new foci on social capital, social enterprise and community cohesion[117] would suggest that the condition of the community itself is the main precondition of involvement.

Community involvement policy now needs to conceive of several strata of involvement. These would include the capacity of individuals, especially those in excluded or deprived situations, to experience themselves as members of the community, to participate in the most rudimentary activities of neighbourly mutual aid and trust[118]. The social capital literature shows that this very basic level of participation is itself a factor in regeneration, and has widespread direct payoffs for the participants[119]:

> 'Crime is strongly negatively predicted by social capital ... the strongest predictor of the murder rate is a low level of social capital ... People are generally less pugnacious where social capital is high ... There is very strong evidence of powerful health effects of social connectedness ... Controlling for your blood chemistry, age, gender, whether or not you have a job and for all other risk factors, your chances of dying over the course of the next year are cut in half by joining one group and cut to a quarter by joining two groups ... No other variable does as well at explaining why states differ in tax evasion. In other words, where people are connected by dense networks of engagement and reciprocity they are more likely to comply with the law, very probably because they are more confident that others will too ... States where people are more connected with each other are also marked by greater tolerance ... Economic inequality and civic inequality are less in states with higher values on the social capital index. Here the causal arrows are likely to run in both directions, with citizens in high social capital states likely to do more to reduce inequalities, and inequalities themselves likely to be socially divisive.'[120]

So local residents are not merely a certain number of people who might become involved in governance but, more fundamentally, also either have, or damagingly lack, networks of acquaintance, small-scale groups, clubs and activities, and the trust that goes with them. The building of basic (bonding and bridging) social capital must therefore in itself be a major factor in regeneration, irrespective of the fact that it can – if other factors allow – also convert into vertical involvement (ie 'linking' social capital). These low-profile but continuous types of interaction are the soil in which vertical involvement capacity grows

---

[117] Local Government Association (2002) *Guidance on Community Cohesion*. London: LGA, DTLR, Home Office and Commission for Racial Equality; Audit Commission (2002) *AC Knowledge – Learning from Audit, Inspection and Research: Equality and Diversity*. Wetherby: Audit Commission Publications; Gilchrist, Alison (2002), *Community Cohesion – Community Development Approaches*. London: CDF (December).

[118] Williams, C and Windebank, J. (1999) *A Helping Hand, Harnessing Self-Help to Combat Social Exclusion*, York: York Publishing Services on behalf of the Joseph Rowntree Foundation.

[119] Putnam, Robert (2000) Bowling alone: *The Collapse and Revival of American Community*. New York: Simon and Schuster; see also *Social Capital and the World Bank*, http://www.worldbank.org/poverty/scapital/bank1.htm

[120] Putnam, Robert (2001), 'Social capital measurement and consequences', *Isuma (US) 2:1, Spring (ISSN 1492-0611)*.

but more importantly they are the texture of local life itself. The absence or sparsity of such networks and activities (often because of the very difficulties which are the subject of regeneration) weighs heavily against both local quality of life and vertical involvement.

The LSP level and the service delivery level of involvement, important though they are, are a superstructure resting on an infrastructure of mutual, lateral relations between people, where people gain more autonomy, more mutually trusting, supportive relations, where the community itself is made more sustainable.

Policy needs to be concerned with both sides of the coin – both vertical and horizontal involvement. To expect 'the community' to act as a coherent player at the level of planning and public services when it is having acute difficulty holding *itself* together, is to divert energies from the place where the impact is 'lived' to the place where policies are made about it. For the people who are immersed in local problems rather than administering them, any contribution to solutions must initially be 'from the inside out' ie an enhancement of their efforts simply to live and flourish in these conditions.

Could government deliberately foster social capital? Philosphically there should be no greater problem with doing so than with its commitment to foster health, education, employment or general wellbeing, all of which remain inalienably the possession of citizens themselves despite state assistance. In practice there is almost bound to be some temptation to try to mobilise and incorporate social capital into government agendas, such as substituting for public services, discussed in the next section. This is not a reason for avoiding the attempt to foster social capital but for vigilance in principles and methods.

A government commitment to build social capital would not be starting from scratch. To some degree this is what community development (also discussed separately below) has attempted to do for the last two generations. The tensions involved in this role, as well as the spasmodic pattern of official support, testify to the paradoxical nature of the endeavour. But it has taken place without the benefit, till very recently, of social capital theory. This could confer greater clarity on practice. Whilst promotion of social capital has always been implicit in community development, the conscious social capital agenda is arguably wider than the typical community development focus, extending on the one hand to social norms and citizenship skills across the whole population (rather than concentrating on experience of disadvantage) and on the other hand reaching further into the quality of personal relationships in the family, household and beyond. Community development practice working to a social capital agenda might pay more attention to forging alliances between disadvantaged neighbourhoods and affluent ones, and between personal identity and capacity for collective action.

4.5 Different types of service

A major boost to policy on capacity building has been given by the Treasury report on the role of the voluntary and community sector in service delivery[121]. However, there is a semantic problem about the term service delivery. Community organisations serve their communities. That is not the same as saying that their role is to deliver part of the public services. We have to think in terms of different types of service. The main service provided

---

[121] H M Treasury, op.cit.

by community organisations is to strengthen community life itself. This was not the subject of the Treasury report but is taken up by two cross-government reviews being carried out by the Active Community Unit of the Home Office: the first on government support for community capacity building; the second on the provision of infrastructural support for both the community and voluntary sectors. It is to be hoped that these will lead to fully complementary measures at the level of supporting basic community activity. These measures could be expected to span both physical amenities, revenue support and community development support.

There are three main types of service provided by the voluntary and community sector:

(i) **autonomous public service** provided by community organisations by means of mutual aid, building social capital, unregulated services and through advocacy and representation of community interests in decision-making arenas. By far the greatest part of the resources going into this role is people's freely-given time and effort. This may be supported by public or private grants, with light touch accountability;

(ii) **specialist services** developed by the voluntary or community sector and then supported with service agreements, contracts or grants by the public sector, with moderate accountability; and

(iii) **statutory public services**, where some part of these has been devolved to the sector by means of contracts or service agreements, with full accountability.

Type (i) may be called **informal or autonomous service**. Types (ii) and (iii) may be called **formal or systematic services**.

It is essential that systematic services and informal service are not confused (even though some organisations may do both). Each should be catered for distinctly in any strategy for government, local government or local partnership relations with the voluntary and community sector.

The role of professionally-led voluntary organisations in delivering statutory or specialist services is an important and growing contribution to public service reform. It is not necessarily, however, in itself, a contribution to community involvement. It might be so by virtue of whether it, in turn, involves local residents actively in decision-making.

The role of community organisations, however, is *primarily* about community involvement – fundamentally 'horizontal' involvement, meaning involvement of local people in community activity. This is virtually synonymous with autonomous service and social capital but is by its nature patchy. It grows 'from the inside out' by the actions of small numbers of people. Strategies to maximise it would need to consist of support to such groups on the scale and in the style of their own motivations, not by trying to turn them into quasi-professional agencies. Techniques of such support are the stock-in-trade of community development, which we discuss below.

Hybrid, or type (ii), forms of service are those where a community or voluntary organisation identifies a need not catered for by the statutory services, both advocates for it and responds to it and then obtains a measure of official support for doing so more thoroughly; or where a public service seeks to enlist the support of community organisations without trying to bind them formally into policy, for example where a health authority refers patients to support groups for particular conditions.

Policy support for greater provision of service by the community and voluntary sector should be sensitive to these gradations, but can face problems of accountability. If increasing sums are handed over without conditions being imposed, what is the guarantee that they will be used in the public interest? But if precise conditions are imposed, how can this avoid demotivating participants and compromising the community group's autonomy? The community enablers scheme introduced by the Living Places policy[122] and endorsed by the Sustainable Communities plan[123] steers a careful course between support and direction. Recognising that people are often motivated to protect and improve the open spaces in their immediate neighbourhood, and noting that over half of English local authorities have no existing green space strategy,[124] the scheme offers small grants to facilitate groups who want to take direct action on this issue, but also lays down some light touch conditions. (See chapter two, section on Living Places and Sustainable Communities, p29fl.)

The provision of community enablers to elicit project proposals and guide implementation is both to help groups access financial support and permission to work on public space and to help them reconcile their self-governing objectives with generalised standards and long-term planning. The enablers, then, are a particular variant of neighbourhood worker, reproducing in this special context the basic community development role.

There has been much debate about whether the community sector and voluntary sector are two parts of the same sector or are separate sectors. Technically and legally there is much overlap but it can easily be seen that there is an extreme divergence in size, function and ethos between most professionally-led voluntary organisations and the (much larger number of) small community-led organisations. The Community Groups Code, a supplement to the Compact between Government and the Voluntary and Community Sector, distinguishes the two ends of the spectrum in such terms as:

- member-led (community groups) as distinct from staff-led;

- less formal structure;

- lower income;

- providing informal and autonomous services rather than specialist and contracted services; and

- representing community interests rather than advocating for client groups.

The great majority of community organisations have very little funding or paid staffing – four fifths have no paid staff at all. Nevertheless, there is continuity along the spectrum, and there are a number of organisations which clearly share characteristics of both types. Indeed, some of the most important community organisations are those which have grown to take on staff and formal service commitments without losing their community ethos and accountability.

---

[122] ODPM (2002) *Living Places – Cleaner, Safer, Greener*. London: ODPM (October).

[123] ODPM (2003), *Sustainable Communities: Building for the Future.* London: ODPM (February).

[124] *Living Places,* p101.

However, whilst it is important for overall quality of life to know the condition of both parts of the sector, for assessing community strength it is particularly important to be able to distinguish the community sector, or the community-driven aspects of multipurpose organisations.

Mature community organisations can be extremely skilled in delivering their own type of public service and eliciting appropriate support from official sources whilst retaining their community identity and autonomy. A framework of seven principles for balancing these roles and applying an appropriate style of quality assurance has been developed by Community Matters for the estimated 4 to 5,000 community associations in England and Wales. The 'visible difference' is summarised as:

Voice: providing a voice for local concerns and for people whose views may not always be heard.

Independent: independent and politically neutral organisations with a powerful commitment to democratic principles.

Service: a provider of services for local people.

Initiator: an initiator of projects that respond to local needs.

Builder: of partnerships with other local organisations and groups.

Local: provide a strong local network of people and organisations woking together and supporting each other.

Engage: provide ways of engaging and encouraging people to become active in their communities.[125]

4.6 Volunteering and public service

All types of service may mobilise some volunteering. Volunteering is rightly seen as a form of service yet is sometimes misleadingly associated primarily with the professionally-led voluntary sector. National surveys of volunteering[126] suggest that rather more volunteering takes place informally, ie outside organisations, than in; and detailed local case studies[127] indicate that as much formal volunteering takes place, hour for hour, in community groups as in professionally-led voluntary organisations. Indeed, since the majority of community groups have no paid staff, these consist entirely of volunteering. Using a classification of seven types of organisation in which volunteering takes place, Marshall's comparative study of 14 localities across Britain produces these proportions[128]:

---

[125] Community Matters (2003), *The Visible Difference*. London: Community Matters (March)

[126] Davis Smith, Justin (1997) *National Survey of Volunteering,* London: Institute for Volunteering Research (includes comparisons with surveys in 1981 and 1991).

[127] Marshall, Tony F. and others (1997), *Local Voluntary Action Surveys* ('LOVAS') London: Home Office, Research and Statistics Directorate. Although the study is now some years old it remains so far the most detailed comparative study available of volunteering in a representative spread of localities in England.

[128] Ibid, LOVAS Paper 3, *Comparing the Areas*, p8.

Category	%
Community and self-help groups	33
Voluntary service organisations	32
Volunteering for religious activity	17
Volunteering based in religious groups	9
Volunteering for statutory agencies	4
Volunteering for schools	4
Community activity in public houses	1
	100

The volunteering that takes place outside any organisation, plus the volunteering in community and self-help groups, ie the majority of all volunteering, would all be mainly providing autonomous service.

The community sector role has not traditionally been regarded as a service because community solutions make the service invisible by dissolving it in mutuality. This is precisely its special value. The merging of provider and beneficiary is the most respectful and empowering form of service. The fact that people are able to participate in community activity, helping others in turn, constitutes the most effective solution to their own problem, reinforcing their autonomy, their sense of giving something back to society rather than merely being dependent on it. Contrary, incidentally, to the familiar demonising of youth, this attitude is a norm for most young people.[129]

The major added value to be found in the sector is not only in mobilising voluntary labour from people who have spare capacity but in turning an inert 'victim' or bystander into an active 'rescuer'. The difference in the person who does the activity is possibly of even greater value to society than the service to the 'client'. The new activist *is* the 'client' whose relation to the community – and the state – is transformed by becoming a provider and governor as well as a beneficiary and subject.

Targeted at small groups, including groups that had never received any funding before, a regional small grants programme[130] illustrates the intimate connections between the autonomous service function of such groups and the daily life of their communities. 73 organisations received awards under a small-grants scheme. These were between them helping several thousand individuals and involving nearly a thousand volunteers. 'Many made reference to the fact that they were run and managed entirely by volunteers and that in some way volunteers were both beneficiaries and mainstays of the organisation ... very few organisations had paid staff. Volunteers were not only running the organisation but delivering services ... In a number of groups the volunteers were closely connected to the client group they were supporting. For example much of the preschool activities were run by the parents, the access groups were run by disabled people, the older people's groups were run by older people as volunteers. Many of the organisations were user-led ... Half the organisations felt the volunteers also benefited, eg. by being involved in the community or by increasing self confidence and self-esteem.'

---

[129] Charities Aid Foundation, *Growing into Giving – Young People's Engagement with Charity*. West Malling, Kent: Charities Aid Foundation, 2002 (Nov).

[130] Crawley, Jan (2003) *Reaching Out*. Bristol: South West Foundation.

4.7 Economic value and the community sector

The role of the community and voluntary sector has a variety of economic aspects. As a provider of contracted public services, the sector is a satellite of the statutory public services themselves – providing public goods at public cost, and generating a certain amount of employment in the process. A second economic role is community enterprise (see below), and a third rests in the hidden economic value of mutual aid, ie autonomous service and social capital. This is perhaps the least understood because it is not transacted through cash.

One reason why community activity is not properly valued is because it is not seen as part of the economy. But this is because 'the economy' is conventionally equated with the cash economy, not the full range of wealth creating action. An image of the complete economy would show both cash and non cash transactions, as in Figure 4.1.

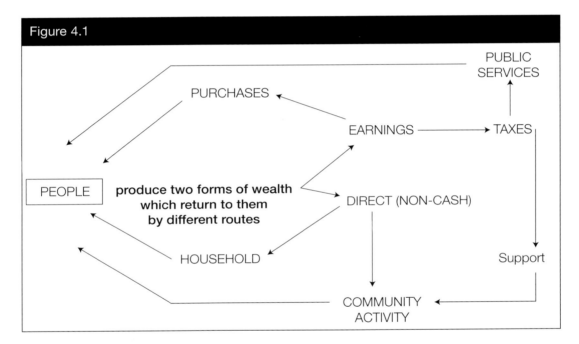

Figure 4.1

Figure 4.1 presents a holistic picture of the economy, with people being both the source of wealth and beneficiaries of it. Their productive efforts take essentially three routes:

a. Earning – purchasing – benefiting from purchases;

b. Paying taxes (both through earning and purchasing) – taxes paying for services – benefiting from services;

c. Unpaid effort with direct (household) and indirect (community) benefit.

Despite the universal experience that this is how personal and economic decisions are made, the conventions dominating public economic discourse ignore the non-cash part of the equation. This directly productive element, however, plays a major support role for society as a whole and therefore for the cash economy as well.

The Office of National Statistics has calculated that the value of unpaid work is about as much again as national GDP. In other words the unpaid economy is as large as the paid one. The great majority of this is household work, including caring, cleaning, washing, cooking, travelling. Volunteering is a relatively minor part of it in terms of sheer volume, but a crucial part in terms of its bridging position between the household and the public sphere.

The professional voluntary sector operates to a considerable extent in the cash economy. Its core work is fully costed and funded, whether through grants, public donations or contracts, but in addition it mobilises a subtantial amount of volunteering, organised as supporting labour.

The community sector, in contrast, operates fundamentally in the reciprocal economy. It does not ask a full cash price for its services, or sometimes any price. This is not because it is cheap, but because it operates a non-cash-based form of supply and demand. In this realm the provider can at any time become the beneficiary and vice versa, or can be both at once. Providers and beneficiaries control the objectives, the operation and the very existence of the activity. It is this that constitutes the real 'glue' that holds society together at the micro level. It is truly voluntary and independent and cannot be subject to market or state criteria. It can however be either facilitated or frustrated by public policies. In particular it needs support in two forms: community development work at neighbourhood level, and a range of propitious physical amenities and conditions.[131]

Between the cash and non-cash economy lies the ambiguous field known as community enterprise. Government guidance defines community enterprise as 'commercial activity…owned and controlled by the community, serving the interests of that community rather than generating private gain…(by) directly or indirectly producing goods or… services for which they charge, and the resulting revenue is their main if not only source of income. It is this which distinguishes community enterprises from the rest of the third or non profit sector of the economy which includes trusts, charities, voluntary and community groups which are funded through donations, endowments and grants rather than trading. But the distinctions are not hard and fast. Many charities obtain a large part of their income through trading subsidiaries.'[132]

This definition places community enterprise firmly in the cash economy. This is not how it is understood by the community entrepreneur movement, which sees community entrepreneurs simply as enterprising individuals who can get things done and generate energy in communities. The community entrepreneur movement is interested in the building of social capital by means of any productive activity, whether transacted by cash or reciprocity.

There are two ways in which this ambiguity matters. Firstly, it matters if it means that community entrepreneurial activities in the reciprocal economy cannot get support even though they are to all intents and purposes the same as community entrepreneurial activities in the cash economy. For example one group of parents may start a youth club, call it a community enterprise, charge fees, employ two part time workers and obtain an enterprise grant. Another group may start a youth club, staff it wholly by their own voluntary effort, charge no fees – and be unable to obtain an enterprise grant. Ironically, the second example would be more economical.

---

[131] Nash, Victoria and Christie, Ian (2003) *Making Sense of Community*, London: Institute for Public Policy Research (IPPR) (February).

[132] DETR (1999) *Community Enterprise Good Practice Guide.* London: ODPM.

The second significance is the widespread conceptual effect of which the first is an example. In order to distinguish community enterprise from 'the rest' of the third sector (including community groups) the guidance defines the rest of the sector's economy as consisting of 'donations, endowments and grants rather than trading'. This omits what is in fact the third sector's main economic resource, namely volunteering. Indeed, it screens out virtually the whole of the community sector. This then is another example of 'the disappearing community' in policy discourse. The limits of the conventional economic model automatically marginalise community.

In informal service what we are looking at is service which is almost synonymous with community activity. If the community does not do it, it does not take place. However, it also has an implicit cash value. A thriving community sector pre-empts some proportion of demand for statutory public services by supporting people in self-sustaining, socially responsible and mutually supportive relationships and networks.

Beyond the immediate household, the ripple of relationships and acquaintance is an important part of the bonds that hold society together. With the ongoing increase in single-person households this can only get more important. Its value is rarely costed because it is freely given. Yet without it far more households and neighbourhoods would be in social and economic crisis, and people would be making heavier demands on public services and benefits. Public expenditure per head of population can be up to 30% more than the national average in cities with major problems of disadvantage, and within such cities public expenditure per head can be up to 45% greater in the most disadvantaged wards than in the least disadvantaged: 'Services which have spending quite strongly skewed towards deprived wards include... social security, social services for children, housing, regeneration and environmental capital spending. Many other services show a more moderate skew in favour of deprived areas: disability benefits, most social services, primary, special and further education, and bus subsidies. Health and secondary education give a relatively flat pattern of per capita spending... and services giving more benefit to affluent areas include higher education, roads, rail subsidies and pensions... Households in the most deprived wards rely for a majority of their real income on public spending.'[133]

Social casualties such as children in care, offenders, homeless people become charges on the state not only because of local economic conditions but also because they have fallen through the network of the community. This implies a huge uncosted economic function of communities in sustaining the great majority of people who do not become social casualties. The economic value of this function can be gauged by the high costs to the state for those who do fall through the community net. The services they require are intensive. (Whether some of these services are then in turn contracted out to voluntary or even community organisations is irrelevant to the preventative economic role of the community sector.)

The claim that the cash economy could not work without the massive silent support of the non-cash economy has been documented in detail by environmentalist and feminist economists.[134] Support to community activity, if effective, pre-empts or reduces some proportion of demand on the paid public services by boosting do-it-yourself social support.

---

[133] DETR (1998) Where Does Public Spending Go? *Regeneration Research Summary No. 20.* London: ODPM. Full report – ISBN 185112.

[134] Eg Waring, Marilyn (1988) *If Women Counted.* London: Macmillan (later republished as Counting for Nothing).

The state role in supporting community activity by means of community development, capacity building and grant aid is of course a cash cost, like other public services. (A line from taxes to community activity in Figure 4.1 acknowledges this.) It would be absurd to use taxes to pay the full cost of community activity – that would in effect turn community activity into a statutory public service. But we should be studying what level of state support to community activity would, without compromising its autonomy, most effectively alleviate the burden on the statutory services.

Such studies might help to overcome the tendency for the intrinsic community role to become marginalised in the economic analysis of social programmes. It could also help to develop models of cost-effectiveness for some kinds of community development practice. It might, further, help to counter the assumption, particularly dominant in European funding, that job creation is virtually the only economic value of third sector involvement in regeneration[135].

4.8 Timescales

One major underlying obstacle to maximising vertical community involvement is the different time perspectives attaching to, on the one hand official development schemes and, on the other hand the growth of community involvement. Community involvement has to grow gradually by a succession of ripple effects. Development planning works through a 'front-loaded' method involving rational planning against objectives, outputs and outcomes which have to be set down at the beginning, and a corresponding budget which has to be spent within time limits. The pressure to spend may come from the top down, before the community is properly on board.

Community involvement literature, on the other hand, often reiterates that community development is not 'a quick fix', but rarely offers much more than this warning in terms of what *can* be expected within a given timescale. This is frustrating to politicians, planners and economists, who need to work within some declared timeframe.

One has to raise the question of whether the way money is allocated to development schemes could not be adjusted, without a major change of financial culture, to fit the trajectory of growing community involvement, rather than to frustrate it. Even without reference to the community as a partner, research carried out for the 'Rethinking Construction' initiative launched in 1998 finds that much waste and inefficiency in public building projects is due to lack of co-ordination among the stakeholders and insufficient lead-in times in planning:[136]

---

135 'The [EU Local Social Capital Pilot] programme originally defined social capital, following Putnam and others, as features of social organisation such as networks, norms and social trust that facilitate coordination and co-operation for mutual benefit. Towards the end of the programme it appeared that Europe was moving the goalposts in terms of projects that it considered eligible ... What they were now solely interested in were projects that could demonstrate a link to the labour market.' Plymouth Community Partnership, op cit.

136 Rethinking Construction, *Rethinking the Construction Client*, London: Rethinking Construction, 2001.

'The nature of traditional projects is to pull together disparate groups of people with different values, aims and objectives who may not have worked together before. Clients are not prepared to pay for projects with long lead-in times despite clear evidence that longer planning periods enable better assessment of risk and reduce health and safety incidents, improve quality and improve delivery cost and time. The underlying reasons for poor performance on traditional contracts stem from the client procurement process. ... The many fragmented layers in the supply chain ... give rise to lack of customer focus. Many organisations have little or no understanding of the end user clients' needs or aspirations. It is this lack of focus on the principal client that gives rise to problems of poor quality products, later delivery and defects. ... The design, planning and costing of a collaborative project should be carried out by an integrated team consisting of the client, main contractor and key suppliers ...'

Much of the professional literature on physical construction over-simplifies not only the client identity but the social purpose of the exercise. Construction industry journals use the term regeneration simply as a metaphor for physical construction projects. 'Paddington station is being regenerated' was the proud legend of placards at that site when the concourse was being rebuilt. In reality, the value of construction projects is intimately connected with whether the community is involved and feels a sense of ownership, as the new planning legislation intends.[137] If local people have been involved in planning, the design and usage are much more likely to fit well with local purposes and achieve high usage and therefore real value; if the community has a sense of ownership, they are more likely to make sure the facility is maintained and protected.

However, even beyond the question of physical amenities, construction projects can contribute to the building of the community itself. Construction projects are an opportunity for leading community members, and through them to some degree for a wider circle of community members, to acquire forward planning skills, negotiation skills and understanding of public finance, with great possible spin-offs in terms of community cohesion, social capital, linking social capital between the community and the authorities and, for some individuals, job prospects. However, for these benefits to be maximised, it is essential that there is recognition of the time implications of the 'ripple effect'.

If one of the main intentions of the new governance arrangements is to provide opportunities for greater community involvement, success will depend highly on getting the right timescales to involve a gradually widening circle of residents.

The community is not a single entity but a series of networks and organisations at differing densities and levels of activity, who can therefore only be involved in a succession of waves. This may mean delaying decisions on some issues till later stages, but the compensating benefit is that by the end of the process the community itself will have been built. This includes the spreading of skills, awareness, networks and trust to wider and wider circles of local people.

We have pointed out earlier the tendency of community involvement guidance literature to use the community to mean anything from a small number of community representatives to specific community groups or the local population as a whole. The loss of clarity in such usage masks the common pattern that, in a given locality, there will be a small number of people and community groups who are aware of local developments, a

---

[137] See 'Planning' in Chapter 2, p33 ff.

penumbra of others who are faintly aware of them and – usually – a majority who are remote. This is quite obvious to the most superficial inquiry in either well-off or disadvantaged communities.

If the aim of community involvement is to involve, ultimately, a sizeable majority, it is quite clear that different strata are at different starting points and will have to go through different stages and timescales. A one-year programme has little chance of reaching beyond the initiated. A five-year programme has a decent chance – if it is structured to do so. Figure 4.2 visualises how this would be likely to apply. We may distinguish for example five strata of the community at different distances from public decision-making:

- organisations with an established policy role, such as the major local umbrella organisations or experienced larger projects which have already been involved in major contracts with the local authority;

- established organisations which have not been involved in this way before;

- smaller groups and organisations which may be less experienced, less professionally resourced and which are unconnected with this kind of development so far – these are likely to be the majority of identifiable organisations in any locality;

- ordinary members of community in their own right, ie local residents;

- local residents who are 'hard to reach' because of greater disadvantage or isolation or conflict with authority.

If we then imagine a development scheme consisting of five stages lasting a year each, experience would suggest a pattern of involvement rippling outwards in the way suggested in the boxes.

Figure 4.2 Crossed wires: stages of involvement for different parts of the community

Stages ▼	Sections of community				
	A	**B**	**C**	**D**	**E**
	Established, policy-aware organisations	Established, policy-distant organisations	Small and unconnected groups and organisations	Average community members	Hard to reach sections, groups and individuals
Planning	Learning how to become involved	Aware but uninvolved	Unaware	Unaware	Unaware
Implementation Stage 1	Involved	Learning how to become involved	Becoming aware	Unaware	Unaware
Implementation Stage 2	Learning how to exercise influence	Involved	Learning how to become involved	Becoming aware	Unaware
Implementation Stage 3	Influential	Learning how to exercise influence	Involved	Learning how to become involved	Becoming aware
Completion	Well positioned for new initiative	Influential	Learning how to exercise influence	Involved	Learning how to become involved

Only the organisations with an established policy role are likely to have a foothold in involvement from the beginning. Even for them, an intensive learning curve would be needed to get fully on board before implementation begins. For other capable organisations, but who have not yet got on this track, it would clearly take a little longer. For the majority of groups and organisations, for most community members, and of course even more so for the 'hard to reach', it is unlikely that they would even be aware of what is going on at the planning stage, and that then it would take several stages for them to become aware, learn how to become involved and eventually become involved, prior to learning how to exercise influence. It is only organisations in the first two categories that have a chance of going through this trajectory and perhaps exercising influence before the completion of the scheme. However, if this natural progression is understood and catered for, projects could be designed, managed and evaluated by their ability to progress each of the strata through the appropriate stages.

4.9 The position of community development

Community development is the main discipline working directly to support community activity and organisation. 'The key purpose of community development work is collectively to bring about social change and justice by working with communities to:

- identify their needs, opportunities, rights and responsibilities;

- plan, organise and take action;

- evaluate the effectiveness and impact of action;

- all in ways which challenge oppression and tackle inequalities'[138]

Community development is central to the community involvement agenda and may even be said to have partly generated it. More importantly, it is an exceptionally relevant source of experience and skills for bringing community involvement about. This is not the place to attempt a history of it[139] but a few key considerations should be brought into the picture.

On the basis of both literature and practice, community development can be considered a continuous movement with a coherent philosophy and established working methods[140] going back at least three or four decades in Britain (and many other parts of the world). The crucial aspect for our purpose here is:

(a) what principles, methods and experience it offers to help engender community involvement against the background of current policy;

(b) how well fitted is its current condition and position for it to play a central part in realising the new community involvement agenda?

Community development practice has often been a combination of sophisticated aims and limited means. Because it necessarily worked through the detailed and the small scale – and was rarely funded for more than this – community development tended to remain low-profile, irrespective of the far-reaching implications of its philosophy. But it grew by accretion and, like the community sector itself, became widely spread without achieving a high profile. This was consonant with its nature but also meant that its policy implications were slow to emerge. Was it community development's failure to articulate itself in the right quarters, or government's failure to appreciate what was going on it in its own back-yard, that made it necessary for the early New Labour government to look for ideas like 'communitarianism' in the United States?[141]

---

[138] Federation of Community Work Training Groups (2002) *The National Occupational Standards in Community Development Work, Summary*. Sheffield: FCWTG, (October).

[139] For a short history see Thomas, David N., (1995) *Community Development at Work, A Case of Obscurity in Accomplishment*. London: Community Development Foundation, Chapter 1.

[140] Eg Henderson, Paul and Thomas, David N., (2002) *Skills in Neighbourhood Work*. London: Routledge (Third Edition); Twelvetrees, Alan (2002), *Community Work*. Basingstoke: Palgrave (Third Edition).

[141] Henderson, Paul and Salmon, Harry (1998) *Signposts to Local Democracy: Local Governance, Communitarianism and Community Development*. London: Community Development Foundation.

Community development has arguably furnished some of the best material available for understanding the complex interactions of communities and authorities. Community development was in fact working on answers to the question of how to promote social capital and sustainable communities at many levels before those concepts were in general currency:

'A critical legacy for a short-life initiative to leave behind is a strengthened community, better able to manage threats and opportunities than it was before. Capacity building of course includes training – developing management skills, expertise and confidence. But it involves much more:

- initial work by short-life agencies with existing community organisations to identify community priorities;

- institutional development – supporting locally-based agencies capable of establishing a long-term presence;

- individual development: not simply training local project managers and activists but ensuring that long term skills development capacity is available in that area;

- infrastructure development – creating networks or umbrella structures to provide support for newer and smaller groups;

- community empowerment to ensure these structures remain responsive to local needs'[142].

Community development theory comes in a variety of strengths. At its most ambitious it sees itself as a catalyst for fundamental transformation of society through the empowerment of the disadvantaged: 'Community development is about building active and sustainable communities based on social justice and mutual respect. It is about changing power structures to remove the barriers that prevent people from participating in the issues that affect their lives.'[143] Sometimes, however, community development is used merely as a rhetorical background to routine social or youth work.

The most intensive deployments of community development, in the 1970s and early 1980s, preceded the evidence-based climate in social policy, and left little legacy of proven outcomes, though a good deal of theoretical literature and project description. A rare long-term perspective on community development exists in the 35 year history of the Community Development Foundation (CDF)[144].

In the 1990s CDF began to introduce more concrete methods of demonstrating outcomes. An evaluation of one of its most substantial local projects, the Wrexham Maelor Community Agency,[145] looked at outcomes of six years' community work by a team of eight, in terms of numbers of community organisations helped and numbers of people

---

[142] GFA Consulting (1996), *Lessons from Inner City Task Force Experience: Good Practice Guide 1, Designing Forward Strategies*. London: GFA Consulting (February).

[143] Standing Conference for Community Development (2001), *Strategic Framework for Community Development*. Sheffield: SCCD (May).

[144] There is no single source for this but see D N Thomas, op cit.

[145] Bell, John (1992) *Community Development Teamwork, Measuring the Impact*. London: Community Development Foundation.

benefitting from the services provided by those organisations. 39 community groups or organisations were helped intensively, 25 of them being started with the help of the project, and a further 93 were assisted occasionally. Main subjects of the groups were tenants and residents, young people, education, unemployment, welfare advice, arts and crafts, health, play facilities, women's issues, elderly people, sports, churches, scouts, community assiocations, skills training and community newspapers. 468 people were intensively involved at one stage or another as committee members or key volunteers and 17,500 people benefitted from the services provided by the groups and organisations. A calculation of total voluntary hours generated by the project showed that overall one hour of paid community work produced 15 hours of volunteering.

An evaluation of a smaller team of four operating in Ogwr from 1989-94[146] gave substantial help to 26 local community and voluntary organisations, nine of them newly started by local residents with the team's assistance, and occasional assistance to a further 48. 355 individuals were intensively involved, and several thousand benefitted from the services.

CDF's portfolio of directly-run local projects was much reduced during the 1990s as a result of government reviews which urged the Foundation to switch more resources into dissemination and policy analysis. Ironically this reduced the immediate application of these innovative methods of evaluation but several pertinent lessons from this period have yet to be digested into community development norms:

(i)   Policy-makers, funders and communities themselves value demonstrable outcomes. The traditional community development (CD) focus on process must not exclude the collection of basic numerical as well as qualitative information which can demonstrate outcomes in conventional policy terms. Much value is hidden by failing to count such things as numbers of people using the services of community groups helped by CD work.

(ii) CD works best where there is a dedicated team deployed on a given patch for a sustained period (3-5 years). Individual workers (whether detached or attached to teams of other disciplines) often feel extremely isolated and cannot mobilise sufficient critical mass to make much impact. Stable long-term teams can achieve much greater-than-incremental outcomes.

Over most of the last generation community development has largely been seen by its employers and funders as a technique to assist particular public services or area-based initiatives. For historical reasons community development as a profession is atomised. Early indications from the first survey of community workers in Britain for two decades[147] show that the profession is poorly structured and poorly paid, and that much of it exists on a piecemeal succession of short term funding. '30% (of respondents) are supervised by someone with no experience in community work... 25% are appointed to posts where neither experience, qualifications nor training in community work is a requirement... and nearly 40% stated that they have to fundraise for their own posts'.[148]

[146] Garratt, Charlie (1994) *Foundations for the Future: Development and Enterprise in a locality under pressure*. London: Community Development Foundation [unpublished].

[147] Standing Conference for Community Development and CDF (2003, forthcoming): *Community Worker Survey*. Sheffield: SCCD and London: CDF.

[148] Henderson, Paul (2003) 'Our survey says', *SCCD News*, 34, Spring 2003. Sheffield: Standing Conference for Community Development. The findings are based on a 'snowball' survey inviting responses from community workers which attracted nearly 3000 responses but may not have captured all types of community work proportionately.

There is nevertheless a considerable community development establishment scattered unevenly through local authorities, health authorities, faith organisations, voluntary organisations and regeneration partnerships.

A useful by-product of the Best Value regime is that a number of local authorities are now examining the deployment of community development across their systems, and potentially, via LSPs, looking also at its deployment across all agencies[149]. Under the impact of community strategies, modernisation and best value, and with the aid, where they can get it, of neighbourhood renewal and regeneration money, councils are re-examining and sometimes repositioning their community development resources.

Community involvement now being a requirement across the board, where should community development strategies be led from? Some councils seem to assume that community involvement merely requires them to be more open in their processes. Others recognise that whether the community can get involved on not depends a good deal on the condition of the local community sector, and that the condition of the sector depends in turn, especially in disadvantaged areas, on community development. But this requires a deployment and and rationalisation of all the community development resources in a locality.

Most authorities are only now beginning to map their community and voluntary sector in a systematic way. Some have a good awareness of organisations which they fund, some of organisations which apply for funding, but few of all organisations[150] and even fewer of the growth and decline of organisations. Local networks funded by the Community Empowerment Fund are surveying their community and voluntary sectors in the 88 special Neighbourhood Renewal areas.[151]

Different service departments within local authorities and other agencies are familiar with 'their' voluntary organisations, very few with the whole voluntary and community sector picture. There is a strong bias towards funding organisations which are providing services that are clearly complementary to the public services themselves: the social capital message that all forms of participation contribute to social cohesion and involvement is not yet influential.

Councils with major regeneration projects tend to be those which already have significant community development establishments. All councils, however, are tending to find that, whether they have used CD much or little, they have used it with very little specific measurement of its outcomes. It has largely been driven, historically, by the enthusiasms of particular departments or officers and by having been found of practical use to assist the delivery of other objectives in some of the main services. Although community development is a key factor in the state of the community and voluntary sector, the connection has rarely been managed in a strategic way.

---

[149] The information on Best Value exercises in the following pages is drawn from unpublished reports held by the authorities mentioned.

[150] Goodall, Richard (2000), *How Many?*, Guildford: Regional Action and Involvement South East (RAISE).

[151] Social Exclusion Unit (2001), *A New Commitment to Neighbourhood Renewal, National Strategy Action Plan*. London: Cabinet Office, SEU (January) Chapter 5 and Annex G suggest that NR schemes should find out 'how much time and money organisations, including community and voluntary groups spend in their areas, and what other assets exist – volunteers, buildings, facilities, organisations, community groups or networks not currently involved in regeneration'.

Specific fractions of neighbourhood renewal money in major urban authorities such as Birmingham, Southwark and Newham are allocated to community work support for area forums, but this is some distance away from the basic neighbourhood work that builds the capacity of the sector.

Assessing the amount and cost of community development that is taking place in a given local authority (a fundamental part of the best value process) is bedevilled by the lack of secure definitions. Authorities vary as to whether their definition of community development includes community-oriented services such as the provision of grants to the voluntary sector, the provision or administration of community centres and support for tenants' associations. The inclusion or exclusion of these makes a large difference to the costing and therefore to the apparent investment in CD. Authorities also differ as to whether to include all grant aid to the sector, aggregated from the different service departments, or only grant aid to community and voluntary sector infrastructure organisations or to community groups.

Sandwell, which 'best valued' its community development in 1999, limited the review to its core CD unit, valued at under £1m a year, and half of this was from temporary sources such as SRB. This was undoubtedly small for an authority of approaching 300,000 people with many very deprived areas, but it excluded CD in main service departments, grants to community and voluntary organisations, community centres, youth work and tenant participation work. It was also just too early to catch neighbourhood renewal/LSPs and area forums. Bradford, for contrast, stated its CD commitment, in 2002, as £14m pa, which included CD by several departments and annual grants to the community and voluntary sector of £3m. Southampton, in 2000, carried out a best value review of 'community involvement services' – its title for many of the activities associated with CD. The service included grant aid to the voluntary sector, support to community groups, support to community centres and the development of area forums but its total investment still only came to £1.14m, not very impressive for a city of about a quarter of a million people with some deprived areas. In a breakdown of cost comparisons on certain criteria it found that it was spending considerably less than Bristol, Coventry or Sandwell on support to community groups and less than Coventry, Newcastle or Sheffield on area or neighbourhood forums.

Southwark began its best value review in 2001 with the intention of reviewing just core community development, which was located in a corporate unit, but then decided to take a much more inclusive approach, calling the area Community Development and Involvement (CDI), to include CD, area forums and voluntary sector support wherever it was located across the authority. Most departments were involved at some level, and the combined investment was identified as £4.6m, similar to several other large London boroughs with deprived areas.

Advocacy of community development by organisations such as the Community Development Foundation and the Standing Conference for Community Development over the years has tended to concentrate on the 'pure' and therefore narrower definition, appearing agnostic about associated questions such as what level of grants a local authority should provide to the voluntary and community sector, to whom and on what criteria, and whether departments should have their own community work establishment or a common pool.

Southwark's invention of the configuration Community Development and Involvement is a sign of the times in that it demands more comprehensive strategy for CD and the associated issues. The Southwark solution of combining community development and involvement represents a modernisation of community development and its merging with the climate of evidence-based policy. The community development orthodoxy of the 70s to 90s that 'it's too important to measure' is being relinquished. It is being realised that measurement, so long as it is appropriate, allows the discipline not only to catch up with public service modernisation but can help to make visible a range of productive activities and social impacts hitherto undervalued – basically the range of effects articulated by theories of social capital.

Can strategic planning, targets and measurement be reconciled with the essentially non-directive methods of community development? 'A networking approach to community development encourages [self-regulatory] processes within civil society, forming links and alliances which provide the requisite conditions for the emergence of community and voluntary organisations. What happens in practice is usually a combination of serendipity and strategy, in which professional interventions play a catalytic but not controlling function... This acknowledgement of chance and emotion is not intended to diminish the influence of policy-makers... or community workers. Rather it highlights the futility of accurate prediction and the need for flexibility around evaluation.'[152]

It does not necessarily follow however that 'community development cannot be realised through business plans or the fulfillment of specific performance criteria' (ibid, p269); rather that business plans and performance criteria should be about such matters as whether networks are formed and strengthened, the volume of community activity and its effectiveness by criteria that are acceptable to local populations and authorities alike, such as the proportion of people who feel they can influence what goes on in their locality, the number of people who help others and the number of people who are active in community organisations (see section on indicators, following) but not in terms of which community organisations should exist, what the organisations should do or what roles individuals should play.

It appears to be endemically difficult for government and large institutions to understand or deal appropriately with the organic nature of the community sector. It is this understanding which is community development's stock-in-trade. But community development is rarely deployed in a sufficiently consistent way to maximise this benefit. The Lighter Touch project[153] found a tendency for funders and professional agencies to assume that small groups were new and wanted to grow, and that their development needed to follow a linear path. Only a small minority of community groups and voluntary organisations, say the researchers, are new or even have a clearly defined beginning. Although some are founded by individual social entrepreneurs, most emerge from informal relationships and occupy an ambiguous space between informal and formal activity, 'the fuzzy frontier': 'They do not necessarily develop, as the ladder theory suggests, along a linear, rational path ... they are dynamic and diverse ... and may be positioned anywhere within the formal/informal spectrum' (p17-18).

[152] Gilchrist, Alison (2000), op cit p269.

[153] Kumar, Sarabajaya and Nunan, Kevin (2002). *A Lighter Touch: An Evaluation of the Governance Project*, York: Joseph Rowntree Foundation and York Publishing Services.

The study also finds that community development support to such organisations was very unstable: 'The groups and organisations either did not have contact, or had lost contact, with any local development workers … The reasons included redundancy, end of short term contracts, restructuring of umbrella groups, unfilled staff vacancies and resignations. … 16 of the 20 organisations were originally assigned a local development worker, but six months later only six organisations were in contact with their worker. … There was a turbulent environment (amongst development agencies)' (p17).

The study by Crawley for a regional grant-making Foundation[154] confirms both the importance and the vulnerability of help from field community workers and umbrella groups. Umbrella groups and community workers were a vital channel for organisations to find out about and apply for the grants. A map of where the grants went showed that they clustered geographically around umbrella groups, councils of voluntary service or development agencies. Where there was no such agency there were large gaps: 'These development workers act as an invaluable resource to those small groups … not only informing them of funding sources but in many cases assisting groups with governance issues in preparation for the application (eg a constitution). The link between funding advice and delivery of grant programmes is clear. However, a number of the funding advice workers are on short term contracts… Areas where there is not a funding advice service or development agency are finding it difficult to access funds from the Foundation. Should the existing advice workers disappear this would only heighten the problems of delivering funds to the smaller, less well networked organisations'.

In short, community development comprises a major resource for the community involvement agenda but one which itself needs substantial upgrading. There is a need for advanced levels of training for strategic community development roles. The profession has largely been recruited from other fields or from direct experience of community activism, and trained through minor options in other disciplines and a variety of short training courses.

An NVQ curriculum for neighbourhood work is available[155], and a number of people have pursued the subject at higher degree level but there is a dearth of mainstream undergraduate courses despite a growing labour market produced by the expansion of regeneration and, more recently, the new governance agenda.

The NVQ standards were produced in 1997 as a basis for Scottish and National Vocational Qualifications at levels 2, 3 and 4. The work was led by the Federation of Community Work Training Groups, and the location of the standards is in 'Paulo', the National Training Organisation for community development work, youth work, and community based adult learning. Paulo is currently in the process of re-forming with other NTOs into a sector skills council, following recent legislation. The revised standards were published in October 2002. The Federation comments: 'Since the first standards were produced in 1997, community development, community involvement, working in partnership, participation etc have become central elements in many government policy initiatives. However, the words are often not reflected or even understood in practice'.

---

[154] Crawley, Jan (2003) *Reaching Out*. Bristol: South West Foundation.

[155] Federation of Community Work Training Groups (2002) *Community Work Occupational Standards*. Sheffield: FCWTG.

The main structure of the standards is formed around six key roles:

(1) developing working relationships with communities and organisations;

(2) encouraging people to work with and learn from each other;

(3) working with people in communities to plan for change and take collective action;

(4) working with people in communities to develop and use frameworks for evaluation;

(5) developing community organisations;

(6) reflecting on development of own practice and role.

There is an urgent need to build on this ground by creating higher levels of community development learning. This should concentrate on the tools necessary to handle strategic levels of community development planning and negotiation in public authorities, other large agencies and major partnerships. Starting qualifications should include successful experience of ground level neighbourhood work and the ability to reflect on it, and further fieldwork should be included in the higher curriculum. This should ensure experience of different perspectives, such as the perspective from within a large corporation, from within a small neighbourhood group, from within a community of interest network such as a black and minority ethnic network, from within a service-providing community organisation, from within a major local partnership, from within a policy-making institution, from within a local community sector umbrella group. Other elements could include:

• understanding the position of community involvement in contemporary policy;

• theory and practice of contemporary governance, including the interactions of local, regional, national and European levels;

• social capital theory;

• organisational development theory;

• operation of CD in specific social areas such as health, housing or employment;

• understanding of public budgeting and the cost benefits of public services;

• understanding the policy-making process;

• international aspects.

4.10 Indicators

If the promotion of community involvement is to become an effective part of public policy, it needs to operate through the same kinds of system that other social policies use, such as behavioural objectives, indicators and targets. There are particular dangers in the application of these instruments to this field which, we have stressed, is essentially autonomous. This paradox has to be faced. What indicators are needed for is not for the state to make judgements on the public but for the public and the state to judge the effectiveness of public policy in eliciting and supporting community involvement.

There are two kinds of safeguard that need to be applied: firstly to remain alert to the danger of creeping state control of citizen action; secondly to ensure that choice of instruments and processes for assessment is made not by government or professional agencies alone but by also by communities themselves. In principle LSPs or area forums would therefore be the right sort of forum to approve these methods. In practice vigilance will be needed there too since most of these forums have yet to establish full credibility as partnerships of equals.

Work is currently taking place on attempts to define indicators of community involvement. A study carried out for the Active Community Unit of the Home Office in 2002[156] assessed whether it was possible to measure attributes of communities. It concluded that it was not possible to measure communities as if they were entities but that it was possible to measure levels and effectiveness of community activity amongst a given population.

The 'ABCD'and 'LEAP'[157] models for evaluating community development produced by the Scottish Centre for Community Development provide pathways for organisations and partnerships to devise their own indicators within a framework of universal values and major public issues.

The Audit Commission ran a working party during 2002 to identify indicators of community involvement to include in the Library of Local Performance Indicators and Quality of Life selection of indicators (with IDeA) which are recommended to local authorities and Local Strategic Partnerships.

The Home Office study concentrated on looking for measures of community life itself, ie the autonomous activities of networks, groups and organisations, not of the many public issues and services *affecting* community life, such as housing, employment, health, crime, environment. The reasoning was that whilst these were clearly major factors affecting the *overall quality of life* of a locality, and whether the community is sustainable, they did not emanate mainly from the community itself and they were already subject to some well-established indicators.

Indicators of community life therefore did not claim to cover the whole of local quality of life but only the major contribution to it of community activity.

---

[156] Chanan, G. (2002) *Measures of Community*. London: Active Community Unit, Home Office, July. Also available from Community Development Foundation and on *www.cdf.org.uk*. A revised edition due in summer 2003 will take account of information here.

[157] Barr, Alan and Hashagen, Stuart (2000) *ABCD (Achieving Better Community Development) Handbook*. London: Community Development Foundation; also *ABCD Trainers' Resource Pack*; Barr, Alan and others (2001) *Learning Evaluation and Planning (LEAP), A Handbook for Partners in Community Learning*. London: Community Development Foundation.

The Home Office study proposed that ideally there would be measurement of 16 factors through a 'triangulated' survey with parallel questions to (a) local residents, (b) community and voluntary organisations and (c) public and professional agencies. The 16 factors were grouped into five clusters:

A. INDIVIDUAL

1. *Self determination*

2. *Concern with locality and/or public issues*

3. *Level of volunteering and community activity*

B. COMMUNITY INVOLVEMENT – HORIZONTAL

4. *Community and voluntary organisations (quantity; range; effectiveness; connectedness)*

5. *Social capital/mutual aid*

C. COMMUNITY INVOLVEMENT – VERTICAL

6. *Voting turnout*

7. *Responses to consultation*

8. *Community representation, leadership and influence*

D. SERVICES AND ECONOMIC ACTIVITY

9. *Contribution to public services*

10. *Social economy and assets*

E. INCLUSION, DIVERSITY AND COHESION

11. *Inclusion*

12. *Diversity*

13. *Cohesion*

F. PROVISION/SUPPORT/EMPOWERMENT

14. *Community development provision*

15. *Community and voluntary sector infrastructure*

16. *Support from partnerships, Neighbourhood Renewal and all public services.*

It was proposed that community strengths should be judged primarily by collecting information on a geographical basis, and that, in urban areas, this could be at the level of a locality somewhat greater than a single neighbourhood and smaller than a whole local authority. It might be necessary, particularly in rural areas, to focus on much smaller settlements such as villages or parishes, where these were felt to be the unit identified with by most residents. However, the principles would apply at any geographical level.

The Audit Commission working party during 2002 identified 27 possible indicators of community involvement and selected four of these as part of the overall Quality of Life set of indicators recommended for use by local authorities and LSPs. These were:

- **QoL 23**: Percentage of adults who feel they can influence decisions affecting their local area;

- **QoL 24**: Extent and influence of local community and voluntary organisations;

- **QoL 25**: Percentage of people who feel that that their local area is a place where people from different backgrounds and communities can get on well together;

- **QoL 26**: Percentage of people who have helped or been helped by others (unpaid and not relatives) once a month or more over the past year.

These are described as 'anchor' indicators for four major factors, respectively

    (1) community influence;

    (2) condition of the community and voluntary sector;

    (3) community cohesion; and

    (4) social capital.

The QoL set also recommended that information for all its indicators be analysable by neighbourhood, ethnic group, gender and ability so that it can be correlated with social inclusion and exclusion.[158]

The four 'anchor' indicators of community involvement in the QoL set are being tested and refined in 2003. It is recognised that they are limited, and users may want to add others to supplement or corroborate them. Additional indicators might be drawn from the other 23 lodged in the Library of Local Performance Indicators.

[158] The Audit Commission QoL indicators were published in Sept 02 in a brochure called *Quality of Life, Public Sector Feedback Paper*, advertised as available on the Audit Commission website or in hard copy from Audit Commission publications, POBox 99, Wetherby, LS23 7JA, phone 0800 502030. The full set of 27 community involvement indicators is accessible at the Library of Local Performance Indicators run jointly by the Audit Commission and IDeA at www.local-pi-library.gov.uk/index.shtml _ community involvement. The four selected for QoL (QoL 23, 24, 25, 26) are numbered there as LIB 137, 138, 139, 140.

QoL 23 and 26, being single questions, are relatively straightforward to collect, and have already been widely used in other contexts. They are based on questions in the first biennial national citizenship survey (Home Office, 2002). QoL 25, on cohesion, was contributed by the Home Office Community Cohesion Unit (CCU), and is the first in a wider set of indicators of community cohesion being idetified by the Unit.

QoL 24 (extent and influence of community and voluntary sector organisations) is more complex and consists of a cluster of six items:

1	Number of voluntary and/or community organisations per 1000 people
2	Percentage of these that are community organisations
3	Percentage of local people who volunteered of played an active role in a community or voluntary organisation at least three times in the past year
4	Range and volume of service provided by the voluntary and community sector in the past year
5	Percentage of professionally-led voluntary organisations who feel they have adequate access to local decision-making
6	Percentage of community organisations who feel they have adequate access to local decision-making

The four Audit Commission community involvement indicators are necessarily limited, bearing in mind the cost of collection and the competing pressures on local authorities and local strategic partnerships. But they have been carefully filtered from a much larger field of options so as to represent *in combination*, a convincing anchorage of evidence. A neighbourhood, locality or village where you can find numerous community and voluntary organisations, a high proportion of people using them, agreement amongst the organisations that they have good access to policy making, and a high proportion of people feeling that they can influence what goes on locally, that they can get on with each other and frequently help each other, can safely be regarded as a place with a high level of community involvement. A place with low counts on all these points can equally safely be regarded as a place with a low level of community involvement.

Of course, it is possible that the findings on these indicators might go in different directions. Local interpretation will always be necessary. Suppose one found many organisations but few people using them. This might point to the organisations not being effective. Suppose one found many organisations and users but few people feeling they had local influence or could get on well with others of different backgrounds. This might point to poor networks between different groupings and organisations, and between organisations and authorities.

Equally significant in the long run will be whether the indicators correlate with indicators on other issues. Current policies affirm that community involvement is essential to improvement of mainstream services and conditions. Since community involvement is mostly not measured, it is impossible to assess this assertion. The neighbourhood renewal system is a case in point: community involvement is fostered through the Community Empowerment Fund, community networks, Community Chests and Community Learning Chests on the grounds that it will assist with the achievement of 'floor targets' in health, housing, employment, education, safety and environment. Yet there is no equivalent to floor targets for community involvement itself, and working out how to measure it has lagged behind the mainstream issues, though it is now in hand.

The positioning of community involvement indicators in the Quality of Life set is therefore of as much interest as simply the fact that they exist. Ultimately we may hope to know, for a particular locality, for a whole city and nationally, such things as whether more community organisations means more informal services, whether more sense of influence on local affairs goes along with more satisfaction with the local area, whether more employment, affordable housing and educational attainment goes along with greater or lesser community activity, and whether more people helping each other goes along with fewer crimes and suicides.

Putting community involvement measures in place would, amongst other things, make possible a more effective deployment of community development and capacity building. If the indicators prove to be meaningful, objectives could be stated in terms of them, as locally determined targets for a specific neighbourhood or area following the establishment of baselines. Variant objectives and indicators could be devised in similar style for more detailed branches of community development, for example the effectiveness of community and voluntary organisations in contributing to particular social issues.

Work continues apace in this field, and there is every prospect that within a few years there will be solid common ground on core and variant indicators of community involvement.[159]

[159] Next steps in the field of CI indicators include a framework for evaluating community capacity building in the Active Community Unit's Community Capacity Building Review, and guidance on testing the Audit Commission CI indicators from the Audit Commission and Community Development Foundation.

CHAPTER 5

Conclusions

5.1 The new localism – prism or illusion?

Critics arraign 'the new localism' for perpetuating the illusion that there can be isolated local solutions to what are in essence national or international problems, and for romanticising the community. This is not at all the approach of the present study. Neighbourhoods and localities rely on frameworks of regional, national and international governance which perform functions essential to their scale. The new emphasis on the local will be self-defeating if it is seen as an alternative to the larger frameworks in which it is embedded. But our relationship with our immediate surroundings is a prism for many of our relationships both near at hand and further afield.

Current lifestyles enable us to some extent to overleap the immediate surroundings and locate ourselves economically, culturally or imaginatively in other types of communities further afield. But in order to do this most of us need a secure anchorage point in a home, a set of personal relationships and a locality. For people with less means the locality is even more important. And at certain times any of us may find ourselves thrown back on the immediate environment more intensively: if we have young children, if we are old, if we are ill, if we are immobile, if we are agoraphobic. What the new governance offers us, and asks us to do, is to voluntarily and proactively perceive the locality as a much more positive vehicle for living and a field for meaningful and fulfilling voluntary action.

5.2 Sorting out meanings

The last ten years' experience of community involvement in urban policy presents a paradox. The subject has been more and more emphasised yet with few clear targets. In some policy documents the imperative for community involvement appears to be fundamental, in others cosmetic. Taking a cross-section, as it were, through the social policies of the last ten years we see the community involvement element generally rising, sometimes falling, moving two steps forward and one step back. Endorsement of community involvement principles now has unprecedented prominence in policy, and some aspects of it have dedicated programme instruments, but key problems of purpose and implementation remain to be resolved.

Government guidance on community involvement has mostly accompanied or formed part of the policies themselves, reflecting the fluctuating meanings. There have been a small number of important guidance landmarks which have reflected a more comprehensive view. New guidance on involvement, including recapitulation of the best of past guidance, would be desirable but presupposes first a clarification of policy itself.

Whilst community involvement has been promoted increasingly in the last ten years there are very few large-scale studies which can tell us how much of it there is and what its effects are. There are however a variety of small-scale researches using varying definitions of the subject. On the whole they show that community involvement is a positive, indeed vital component of urban development but that it faces tough obstacles in the disadvantaged areas where it is most needed. Policies on community involvement now having reached a critical mass, government and others are asking with some urgency how much of it there is, what it consists of and what its effects are.

There is no doubting the seriousness of the government's vision regarding community involvement. What causes it to disappear from view intermittently is a lack of clarity about what it is, and consequently a lack of distinct objectives, funding and measurement. Four meanings intermittently reappear in different conflations:

The dominant meaning in policy (meaning **A**) is that community involvement is **the involvement of local residents in governance** of regeneration plans, renewal strategy, LSPs or area or neighbourhood forums. This is elsewhere called linking social capital, or vertical involvement.

The second meaning (**B**) is **the involvement of community or voluntary organisations in delivering public services**.

This meaning itself has three branching meanings which are often confused:

> **B(i)**: community or voluntary organisations bidding for contracts to deliver part of a **statutory service**, and accepting the standards and regulations that go with that;

> **B(ii)**: community or voluntary organisations delivering **a specialist professionally-led service** for which they obtain grant aid and accept a degree of regulation;

> **B(iii)**: community or voluntary organisations providing **service by their own choice** and effort, to their own objectives, mostly through voluntary activity but which may also seek grant aid because it is of public benefit.

B(i) diversifies the range of statutory service providers. B(ii) diversifies the range of specialist services. B(iii) strengthens communities and increases social capital.

The third meaning (**C**) is the **involvement of individuals in community activity**, from wholly informal friendship networks to volunteering in community or voluntary organisations. This is the foundation of social capital and merges into B(iii).

The fourth meaning (**D**) is **community enterprise**, ie commercial activity with social goals, usually through a non-profit-making business (Community enterprise in the general, non-commercial sense is part of B(iii) and C).

5.3 Slippery meanings weaken impact

Scanning the series of policies which invoke community involvement provides some fairly clear indications of why community involvement has had difficulty in becoming successfully embedded:

Most government guidance and funding focuses on meaning A above (governance) and meaning B(i), devolving the delivery of statutory services. There is rarely any clear distinction between B(i), B(ii) and B(iii), and there is little policy which prioritises (C) capacity-building of the community sector as a major regeneration goal in itself, ie to boost social capital at its roots. However, this is the subject of a current cross-government inquiry led by the Active Community Unit of the Home Office.

The condition of the community sector is not itself usually noticed as a feature of disadvantage, and is therefore only brought into the picture at the point where involvement is sought. Consequently, involvement continues to be seen merely as a method to achieve other objectives, lacking criteria of its own.

Another fairly simple but material factor in the periodic 'disappearance' of community in the policy stream is the probability that as programmes move from principles to action plans and from action plans to implementation and are handed on from one level to another, the recipients concentrate primarily on the structured and budgeted points and not on the matters of vision and principle, however fulsomely expressed.

There are also legitimate and necessary divergencies regarding what community involvement means in specific policy areas. Major public services like education, health, planning each have their own uses for it, which cannot be reduced to a single mechanism even though they all call on the same underlying principle. The much-echoed call for joined-up government cannot sensibly abolish necessary specialisms and sectoral responsibilities. The different major public services properly relate to different aspects of communities and therefore, to some extent, to different community and voluntary groups and organisations. Each of these major public services has its own professional subculture within which the principle of community involvement has to be designed to reflect the specific responsibilities and methods of that service. There has been vigorous policy-specific development of ideas on community involvement in most of the major fields such as health, education, housing and planning.

The National Strategy for Neighbourhood Renewal made a step change on this issue by structuring in development support for the sector at several levels. It still, however, focused primarily on the top end of vertical involvement: the community sector is supported mainly to help it get involved in the LSP. Although the strategy provides scope for setting targets of community involvement and community sector progress it falls just short of requiring it. In practice, community involvement in the neighbourhood renewal system may be in danger of continuing to be squeezed to the margins by the imperatives of the five or six main floor targets.

To complete the circle, it needs to be recognised that a poor condition of the community sector, reflecting the poor condition of community life, is also a measure of disadvantage, and one that needs targets. The damage suffered by localities which lose employment, where housing is poor, where education, health and other major social issues are in a bad state is suffered also by the community sector, ie the capacity of the local community to engage in constructive collective activities. The community sector as a whole is likely to have been weakened in precisely those places where its role is now most wanted.

5.4 Flexibility and targets

There is another more complex factor that may also aggravate the periodic fluctuation of the community element in policy, and between policy and implementation. Involvement is highly approved in principle but at the same time government and authorities have a clear obligation to base regeneration and public service plans on the best objective information they can obtain, and so, in the unfolding of programmes, participation can get pushed to the sidelines. This is not merely a cultural feature of bureaucracies, though that plays its part. It is to some degree an objective problem of different requirements placed on government by society as a whole. We want involvement and innovation but we also want measured improvements on well-known issues.

We have seen policy struggling to reconcile community involvement with objective social issue targets. Urban policies and area-based initiatives are driven by a combination of popular discontent and statistical evidence of deprivation. The statistical evidence, eg the ODPM indices of deprivation,[160] explains to a considerable degree why stress – and therefore intensive demand on public services – is concentrated in some local areas far more than in others. It is therefore rational to direct certain extra resources to those areas and also to the particular issues on which the statistics show those areas to be markedly poorer than the norm. The establishment of government targets on those issues, within the overall aspiration that in twenty years' time no-one should be disadvantaged by where they live, is a clear advance on simply 'throwing money at the problem' as previous policies had frequently been accused of doing. But if targets are imposed from above and based on objective calculations, what influence can local people have on the choice of objectives and design of schemes?

Over the years, and across different administrations, we see government struggling with this paradox, at times emphasising one side of it, at times another. New Deal for Communities offered total flexibility of scheme objectives in order to maximise involvement. The National Strategy for Neighbourhood Renewal as a whole, however, imposed obligatory priority issues and objective targets. Community strategies emphasise the leading role of the community. But the White Paper of December 2000 emphasises local authority leadership and has little to say about community involvement. The Treasury cross-cutting review on the role of community and voluntary sector fuels capacity-building plans for service delivery and monitoring by the sector, but not for the general growth and strengthening of the community.

We would propose that the answer lies in distinguishing more clearly the four elements of involvement that we clarified above, and treating them as distinct policy objectives to be balanced in specific schemes.

Strategies should recognise that whilst it is in the nature of much community activity to provide service to others, that service remains freely chosen and freely given and cannot therefore, so long as it is truly community-driven, be wholly systematic or accountable to public sector norms.

---

[160] DETR (2000), *Indices of Deprivation 2000*, Regeneration Research Summary 31. London: DETR.

Whilst the building up of service provision by the professional voluntary sector is an objective in its own right, and whilst there is some natural cross-over from community organisations to professional voluntary organisations, the role of the latter must not be substituted for the strengthening of the community itself.

But it should also be recognised that meaningful involvement in specialist areas such as the major public services can require a high level of expertise and continuity, which can only be expected from a small number of community members and experienced groups. An involved community will need to contain a number of long-term specialist groups. Strategies should therefore foster both the necessary expertise and the capacity of the community's own experts to communicate with local residents as a whole, to nurture newcomers who could boost their number and to communicate and link up across specialisms to create a network of expertise across public issues.

5.5   Salience in policy

The main casualty of unclear policy is horizontal community involvement. Because of the policy preoccupation with service provision and the dilemmas of governance, the question of how to involve the majority of people in community activities is neglected so long as it is assumed to be part of the same bundle of objectives. But it is a different issue. It is about the fundamental basis of social capital: how many people, and which people, are involved in constructive community activities; how many community groups and organisations are there in the locality; how accessible are they to the most disadvantaged people; how many pathways are there for people to meet new friends, carry out fulfilling activities, make bridges to people they are unfamiliar with; what additional, non-statutory, services are provided?

These activities can ultimately feed vertical participation as well. Indeed vertical participation cannot happen without them. But their primary purpose and overwhelming motivation is much closer at hand: it is the participation itself that is beneficial. People go to a local sports club, choir, social club or the social and welfare activities run by faith organisations because the activity is enjoyable and meaningful to them in its own right. Its possible connection with local governance may be of background interest or no interest – it is rarely the main purpose. Indeed, it would be disproportionate to the whole operation of the sector if it *were* the main purpose. Yet, as the social capital literature shows, all this horizontal participation has hugely beneficial effects on all the main issues that are addressed by the public services. Conversely, the decline of such participation in a particular locality may herald crisis in education, health, crime, happiness in general and even payment of taxes.

The idea of social capital is now well known in government and local government but it has as yet no clear home. In central government, the idea of social capital has been championed by the Strategy Unit but with no obvious implementation arm. The space for a social capital policy is already partly occupied by the variety of policies on community involvement, so any major new initiative on social capital would need to both clarify and build on these.

Much policy discourse has seen the main value of the community and voluntary sector as being the delivery of supplementary public services. This function is suitable for professionally-led voluntary organisations. It may also be suitable as an additional activity by some community organisations. However, the greater the role that community organisations take in systematic services the less difference there is between them and the public services *per se,* and the greater the distance between them and community-led activity. Ironically, if the whole community and voluntary sector were to be diverted to help provide public services, the services might be greatly boosted but the need for them would escalate beyond reach as communities collapsed for lack of basic social capital.

The image of the sector in the media often reflects the confusion of these roles. In a *Newsnight* item on 12 Feb 03 (BBC2 TV) the strengthening of communities was seamlessly identified with the notion that public services could be devolved to the voluntary sector. On the rather rare occasions when issues about community involvement surface in the mass media, even the serious media, they are almost invariably treated as simply being about volunteering, interpreted as the mobilisation of free labour to assist public services. It seems impossible that more complex government intentions will come across clearly without a specific media campaign to establish the value of community activity in building social capital, overcoming exclusion and strengthening democracy.

5.6   Establishing balanced objectives

The answer to the confusion of aims is not blanket flexibility but a clear distinction of the five roles of the sector and the establishment of different types of objective and criteria for each role.

By separating out the area of social capital, which is in itself vital to the health of society, policy could set clear targets for improvement in this area without confusing this with the need for the statutory services. But targets for the overall level and vigour of social capital should have the same status, resource pathways and treatment in social policy as do traditional social issues such as health, housing and jobs. We need neighbourhoods that have *demonstrable* improvements in employment, health, housing, safety, education *and social capital*. It is only by building this into policy in the same style as the established issues that we can ensure that it does not evaporate in practice.

The criteria for delivery of public services are already laid down in those services. There may be specific added value from the use of community or voluntary organisations, such as greater user involvement, a more personal touch, a more welcoming style. There cannot however be any guarantee that community or voluntary organisations automatically provide these better than others. These are therefore not community or voluntary criteria as such but general service delivery criteria for which community and voluntary organisations may simply be in a good position to compete.

For community enterprise defined as commercial activity, goals could be set regarding the volume of this type of activity that should be achieved. For the other meaning of community enterprise, an enterprising approach to community activity – the goals are inherent in general social capital goals.

For vertical participation (governance) goals could be set in terms of levels of local voting, numbers of community representatives on partnerships, the ways that partnerships should support and incorporate those representatives, the ways those roles should be legitimated, how they should complement, not compete with, the role of local councillors, how they should be held accountable, how their effectiveness should be judged, how they should communicate with their constituencies. Models for these types of criteria are available.[161]

Horizontal participation is the largest and most neglected area and here the objectives should be in terms of bonding and bridging social capital: how much social interaction people have, how much volunteering (both in and out of organisations), how many people take roles of responsibility in community groups and organisations, how many activities are regularly available to local people, what range of activities is covered.

Since it takes a group or organisation of some sort to sustain regular activities, groups and organisations are important for social capital. They are also important for the opportunities they provide for people to participate actively. It may take only three people to administer a sports club with hundreds of members, but scores of those members are often involved in arranging matches. There may also be a connection with vertical involvement, for example if a committee member attends a local forum in order to protect its interests or press for a new playing field in the neighbourhood.

Most such groups are therefore also providing some public service, but what these are must remain in their own hands. Virtually all the public service generated by the community sector is of value to local development, indeed *is* local development. But it can only be measured post-hoc. What policy should do in this area is to support it through community development, provision of amenities, small but regular facilitating grants, administrative support, information and publicity. Outcomes here should be measured in terms of volume of activity, satisfaction of participants, sections of the community participating, variety of autonomous services provided.

5.7 Converting social capital – linking with governance

The community sector itself is not always well mobilised. Most community organisations consist of individuals who are preoccupied with the issue they have taken up. When opportunities arise for dialogue about local development their priority is naturally to press for the cause they are concerned with. Other than in the umbrella groups, there is little tradition of advocating for the role of the sector generically, even though all groups are always looking for more volunteers, more understanding of their situation and more funding. Yet the umbrella groups are often quite small organisations themselves, often smaller than some of the better-resourced of their local members, and their agendas may be dominated by those members. They may also feel too closely tied to local authority discretionary grants to develop independent policies. The CVSs and RCCs themselves generally recognise that whilst they have the scope to carry out a strategic community development role their ability to do so is in reality very variable.

---

[161] Eg COGS (2000), *Active Partners, Benchmarking Community Participation in Regeneration*. Leeds: Yorkshire Forward; Burns, Danny and Taylor, Marilyn (2000) *Auditing Community Participation*, York: Policy Press for the Joseph Rowntree Foundation.

Other local organisations which take up governance issues – town centre improvement groups residents' associations, police-community liaison groups, environmentalist groups – are important vehicles for conversion of 'pure' social capital into governance (or of bonding and bridging social capital into linking). This is a natural potential for many community and voluntary organisations as one aspect of their activity though often not realised.

If local communities are to rise to the present opportunities there has to be a large amount of network development and micro organisational development, and more consciousness of the potential interactions between bonding, bridging and linking social capital and what factors favour conversion of one into another. This indicates a need for progressive, multi-faceted development within the community and voluntary sector itself; in turn requiring sustained and co-ordinated community development input, rather than the fragmented and intermittent input which seems to be too common.

5.8 Reconfiguring community development

The community development (CD) profession offers some of the essential concepts and practices to develop community involvement in all its senses, but itself needs development to fill gaps and raise its capacity. CD theory and aspirations were ahead of their time in putting forward principles of community involvement long before they were prominent in public policy. At the level of practice, experience has been largely through small short-term projects and auxiliary departmental roles. Community development has also been associated at times with an adversarial attitude towards government and local government which may have impeded its legitimate influence.

The community development profession is in some disarray. The first survey of community workers for two decades shows that the profession is disorganised, low paid and insecure. There is little dedicated training in what might be called strategic CD. Notably there are very few first degree courses which take up this agenda. There is a shortage of people who can authentically lead CD teams and networks and negotiate strongly to inject a CD perspective into local development partnerships and schemes. Such people would need to have both substantial CD field experience, an up-to-date awareness of policy contexts and a modernised, evidence-based approach to strategy. High levels of skill are needed both at the front line – in neighbourhood work – and in strategic planning and managing of CD in local authorities, LSPs, Primary Care Trusts and throughout the public services. In the absence of effective standards in these roles, major responsibilities and opportunities are being distributed haphazardly. A generation of people is needed with the vision and skills to organise neighbourhood work, co-ordinate it across localities and guide major authorities and agencies in developing CD strategies and relating CD to the modernisation and new governance agenda.

5.9 Conclusion

Overall, the central finding of this report is that Government should continue to promote community involvement throughout social and economic policy, and particularly through active community policies, urban and rural development, the modernisation of local government, local community strategies, local strategic partnerships, neighbourhood renewal, tenant management, regional development, the planning system, the living places policy, the sustainable communities plan, the reforms of the health system, citizenship and civil renewal policies, community cohesion, community enterprise, and citizenship education in the school curriculum, Connexions and adult education.

Community development and capacity-building effort in local authorities, neighbourhood renewal and other programmes should be directed to appropriate combinations of community involvement objectives, balancing the generic aims of community involvement, the distinct aims of particular programmes and the aims of different types of public service.

Criteria for social capital and autonomous service should be in such terms as levels of volunteering, mutual aid, trust and co-operation and community cohesion, making use of measures of these factors such as those being established by the Audit Commission, the Community Cohesion Unit, the national citizenship survey, the Office of National Statistics and the Active Community Unit's current reviews of community capacity building and community and voluntary sector infrastructure.

Distinct criteria should, similarly, be developed for the other objectives: involvement in public decision-making and monitoring of public services; provision of (different types of) service by community and voluntary organisations; and facilitating the contribution of communities to building up local economic activity and social enterprise.

The concluding pages which follow contain ten recommendations to move this agenda forward.

Recommendations

1. ODPM should, in consultation with the Active Community Unit, produce a statement of the objectives of community involvement across the field of local government, housing, neighbourhood renewal and urban and regional development, drawing together the best of the principles and instruments already embedded in recent ODPM policy such as the Urban White Paper, Community Strategies, Planning reforms and the Living Places programme, and taking account of the ACU's current cross-government reviews of community capacity building and capacity building and infrastructure. This should also take account of other key issues and departments such as DEFRA to ensure the inclusion of the rural perspective, DoH on health aspects and DfES on educational aspects.

    Once strategy for community involvement has been clarified in such ways as those recommended above, new guidance on it should be produced, showing the common criteria across government and signposting the distinct criteria of specific programmes. This should also recapitulate those parts of previous guidance from 1995 onwards that are still relevant.

2. Government should promote a better understanding and appreciation of its community involvement policies and achievements in the media.

3. Objectives and methods of improving community involvement at both national, regional and local level should include but clearly distinguish between:

    (a) building up social capital and community cohesion in local communities;

    (b) maximising local residents' engagement and involvement in public decision-making and monitoring of services;

    (c) facilitating different types of service provision by community and voluntary organisations;

    (d) facilitating the contribution of communities to building up local economic activity and social enterprise.

4. A clear distinction should be made between different types of service provision by community and voluntary organisations and the different criteria to be applied to them, namely:

    (a) mutual aid, autonomous public service and opportunities for personal involvement in community activity, which should be supported and stimulated by policy on the arm's-length principle, through community development, capacity building and wide distribution of small grants, in order to strengthen social capital and community cohesion;

    (b) parts of public services contracted from public authorities, which should be supported and stimulated but subject to normal standards and accountability of public service;

(c) hybrid forms where for example public programmes such as Living Places seek to stimulate community involvement through quasi-autonomous service within a public service framework with light-touch criteria.

5. ODPM and ACU should jointly consider the feasibility of a national review of community development and capacity building at local level, taking account of the Active Community Unit's current reviews of community capacity building and infrastructure, with a view to better local co-ordination of input from different agencies, establishing criteria of success and filling any serious gaps in provision.

6. Community-related programmes should include a guideline on proportion of local budgets to be invested in community development and capacity building for community involvement, such as the 10% guideline used in the last two rounds of the Single Regeneration Budget.

7. Baselines and targets for community involvement and social capital should be considered in Neighbourhood Renewal alongside the existing floor targets.

8. Levels of community involvement should be added to the national and regional headline sustainability indicators.

9. Research should be carried out on continuing issues of community involvement either jointly or by arrangement between the Home Office, ODPM, the Department of Health, DfES the Cabinet Office and other departments, and severally by them on departmentally specific aspects. Key issues to be considered include:

    • the relationship between horizontal mass involvement in general community activity and the vertical involvement of community representatives in governance;

    • the effects of differential social and economic change in different localities on the capacity of the community and voluntary sector to operate effectively;

    • the different types of challenge faced by the community and voluntary sector in different types of urban and rural context such as ex-industrial areas, new settlements, areas of population decline and areas of intensive development;

    • the levels of community involvement of different types actually being achieved and their effects on social capital, on public service objectives and on local quality of life;

    • the cost-benefits of the effect of supporting autonomous community activity on better community cohesion and relief of pressure on public services (possibly through the invest-to-save programme).

10. Government should press for European social policies, in particular the next period of the Structural Funds, to adopt the principles and types of method advanced in recent community involvement policies in the UK.

Sources and references

Animation and research (1994). *Poverty 3, Developments and Achievements. Central Unit Report, Fourth period.* Lille: EEIG Animation and Research.

Arnstein, S. (1969) 'A ladder of citizen participation in the USA', *Journal of the American Institute of Planners*, July.

Atkinson, Dick (2000), *Urban Renaissance: A Strategy for Neighbourhood Renewal and the Welfare Society.* Studley, Warwickshire: Brewin Books Ltd (April).

Audit Commission (2002), *Policy Focus, Neighbourhood Renewal,* London: Audit Commission.

Audit Commission (2002) *Quality of Life, Public Sector Feedback Paper*, Wetherby: Audit Commission Publications (October) and www.local-pi-library.gov.uk/index.shtml.

Audit Commission (2002) *AC Knowledge – Learning from Audit, Inspection and Research: Equality and Diversity.* Wetherby: Audit Commission Publications.

Bell, John (1992) *Community Development Teamwork, Measuring the Impact.* London: Community Development Foundation.

Burns, Danny and Taylor, Marilyn (2000) *Auditing Community Participation,* York: Policy Press for the Joseph Rowntree Foundation.

Burrows, Roger (2003) *Poverty and Home Ownership in Contemporary Britain.* Abingdon: The Policy Press (January).

Chanan, Gabriel (1999), *Local Community Involvement, A Guide to Good Practice.* Dublin: European Foundation for the Improvement of Living and Working Conditions.

Chanan, G., Garratt, C. and West, A. (2000), *The New Community Strategies, How to Involve Local People.* London: Community Development Foundation.

Chanan, Gabriel (2002) *Measures of Community.* London: Active Community Unit (Home Office) and Community Development Foundation (July).

Charities Aid Foundation (2002), *Growing into Giving – Young People's Engagement with Charity.* West Malling, Kent: Charities Aid Foundation (November).

Chelliah, Ramani (1995), *Race and Regeneration, A Consultation Document,* London: Local Government Information Unit.

Church, Chris (2002) *The Quiet Revolution.* Birmingham: Shell Better Britain Campaign.

Church, Chris and Elster, Jake (2002) *Thinking Locally, Acting Nationally: Lessons for Policy from Local Action on Sustainable Development.* York: York Publishing Services for the Joseph Rowntree Foundation, and London: Community Development Foundation.

COGS (2000), *Active Partners, Benchmarking Community Participation in Regeneration.* Leeds: Yorkshire Forward.

Community Development Foundation (1997), *Regeneration and the Community, Guidelines to the Community Involvement Aspect of the SRB Challenge Fund*, London: CDF (April).

Community Matters (2003), *The Visible Difference.* London: Community Matters (March).

Coulton, C J (1998), *Comprehensive Approaches to Distressed Neighbourhoods in the United States*, Dublin: European Foundation and Paris: OECD.

Crawley, Jan (2003) *Reaching Out.* Bristol: South West Foundation.

Davis Smith, Justin (1997) *National Survey of Volunteering*, London: Institute for Volunteering Research.

Department of Health (2000) *The NHS Plan*, London: DoH (July), and *The NHS Plan, A Summary.* Also at: www.nhs.uk/nationalplan/summary.htm

Department of Health (2002), *Commission for Patient and Public Involvement in Health (Functions) Regulations, Consultation Document*, London: Department of Health (September) See also www.doh.gov.uk/cppihconsultation.

DETR (2000), *Our Towns and Cities: the Future. Delivering an Urban Renaissance.* London: ODPM.

DETR (1997), *Involving Communities in Urban and Rural Regeneration.* London: ODPM. Revised edition.

DETR (1999), *New Deal for Communities, Race Equality Guidance.* London: ODPM.

DETR (1998), *Single Regeneration Budget Bidding Guidance Round 5.* London: ODPM.

DTLR (2001), *Strong Local Leadership, Quality Public Services.* London: ODPM.

DETR (1998), *New Deal for Communities Phase 1 Proposals, Guidance for Pathfinder Applicants.* London: ODPM.

DETR (2000), *Preparing Community Strategies, Government Guidance to Local Authorities.* London: ODPM.

DETR (1999), *A Better Quality of Life. A Strategy for Sustainable Development for the United Kingdom.* London: ODPM.

DETR (1999), *Community Enterprise Good Practice Guide.* London: ODPM.

DETR (2001), *Our Towns and Cities: The Future, Implementation Plan.* London: ODPM.

DETR (2001), *Local Strategic Partnerships, Government Guidance*. London: ODPM.

DETR (1997), *Effective Partnerships, A Handbook for Members of SRB Partnerships* London: ODPM.

DETR (1998), *Modernising Local Government, Improving Local Services Through Best Value*, London: ODPM.

DETR (1998), *Urban Exchange Initiative*, London: ODPM.

DETR (1999), *Draft New Deal for Communities Race Equality Guidance*, London: ODPM.

DETR (1999), *Urban Renaissance: Sharing the Vision, Summary of Responses to the Urban Task Force Prospectus*, London: ODPM.

DETR (2000), *Guidance on Preparing Regional Sustainable Development Frameworks*, London: ODPM.

DETR (2000), *Preparing Community Strategies, Draft Guidance to Local Authorities*, London: ODPM.

DETR (1995), *Involving Communities in Urban & Rural Regeneration, A Guide for Practioners*, London: Partners in Regeneration, ODPM.

DETR KPMG (1998), *Final evaluation of City Challenge: What works – emerging lessons for urban regeneration*. London: ODPM.

DETR (1998), *Where Does Public Spending Go?* Regeneration Research Summary No. 20. London: ODPM

DETR (2001), *Planning: Delivering a Fundamental Change* (Green paper). London: ODPM.

DoE (1995), *SRB Challenge Fund, Guidance Note 1*. London: ODPM.

Donzelot, J and Jaillet, M (1997), *Deprived Urban Areas, Summary Report of Pilot Study*, Toulouse: Centre Interdisciplinaire d'Etudes Urbaines.

European Commission (1997), *Community Involvement In Urban Regeneration: Added Value and Changing Values*, Luxembourg: Office for Official Publications of the European Communities.

European Commission (1998), *Sustainable Urban Development in the European Union: A Framework for Action*. Brussels: European Commission.

Federation of Community Work Training Groups (2002), *The National Occupational Standards in Community Development Work, Summary*. Sheffield: FCWTG, (October).

Fittall, W (Chair) (1999), *Report of the Policy Action Team on Community Self-Help* ('PAT 9'). London: Home Office, Active Community Unit (September).

Garratt, Charlie (1994), *Foundations for the Future: Development and Enterprise in a locality under pressure*. London: Community Development Foundation [unpublished]

Garnett, T. and Richardson, L. (1999), *What's Regeneration All About, A Guide to Government Funding in the Community*, Trafford: National Tenants Resource Centre.

Geis, Karlyn J. and Ross, Catherine E, (1998) 'A new look at urban alienation: the effect of neighbourhood disorder on perceived powerlessness', *Social Psychology Quarterly* (US), 61:3.

GFA Consulting (1996), *Lessons from Inner City Task Force Experience: Good Practice Guide 1, Designing Forward Strategies*. London: GFA Consulting (February).

Giddens, Anthony (1991), *The Consequences of Modernity*, Cambridge: Polity Press.

Gilchrist, Alison (2000): 'The well-connected community: networking to 'the edge of chaos''. Oxford: Oxford University Press: *Community Development Journal*, 35:3, July, pp 265-269.

Gilchrist, Alison (2002), *Community Cohesion – Community Development Approaches*. London: CDF (December).

Gillan, Audrey (2002), 'Where the law abiding live in fear'. *The Guardian*, November 11.

Goodall, Richard (2000), *How Many?*, Guildford: Regional Action and Involvement South East (RAISE).

Henderson, Paul and Salmon, Harry (1998), *Signposts to Local Democracy: Local Governance, Communitarianism and Community Development*. London: Community Development Foundation.

Henderson, Paul and Thomas, David N., (2002), *Skills in Neighbourhood Work*. London: Routledge (Third Edition).

Home Office (1998), *Compact on Relations between Government and the Voluntary and Community Sectors in England*. London: Home Office (November).

Home Office (2001), *Building Cohesive Communities*. Ministerial group on public order and community cohesion (Denham report). London: Home Office.

Home Office (2001), *Community Cohesion, Report of the Independent Review Team* (Cantle report). London: Home Office.

H M Treasury (2002), *The Role of the Voluntary and Community Sector in Service Delivery*. London: H M Treasury (Sept).

Kamat, Anita (2001), *Room for Growth, Patterns and Potential in Black and Minority Ethnic Volunteering*. Bristol: Black Development Agency and London: Community Development Foundation.

Kings Fund (2001), *What's to Stop Us?* London: Kings Fund (December).

Knock, M. and Zahno, K (1999), *Capacity Building, The Way Forward*, London: London Regeneration Network.

Kumar, Sarabajaya and Nunan, Kevin (2002). *A Lighter Touch: An Evaluation of the Governance Project*, York: Joseph Rowntree Foundation and York Publishing Services.

Kyprianou, Paul (1999), *Community Participation and Partnership, A Review of Participation in the Liverpool Objective One Partnerships*. Liverpool: Liverpool Euro Community Network.

Lawless, Paul et al (2000), *A Review of the Evidence Base for Regeneration Policy and Practice*, London: ODPM/ www.urban.odpm.gov.uk/research/summaries/03900/index.htm

Local Government Association, ODPM, Home Office and CRE (2002) *Guidance on Community Cohesion*. London: LGA

Lowndes, Vivien and others (1998), *Modern Local Government: Guidance on Enhancing Public Participation*. London: DETR (now ODPM) (October).

Lowndes, Vivien et al (2002), *Social Capital and Political Participation: How do Local Institutions Constrain or Enable the Mobilisation of Social Capital?* Paper for Cambridge Social Capital Seminar, 19 November.

Lucas, Karen, Ross, Andrew and Fuller, Sara (2002), *There's more than one way to skin a cat – From Local Agenda 21 to Community Planning and Beyond*. London: University of Westminster, Centre for Sustainable Development (October).

MacFadyen, Ann (2002), *Engaging with Communities: Disentangling Government Policy and Programmes that Impact on local NHS Organisations and Community Engagement*. London: Dept of Health (September).

MacFarlane, Richard (1993), *Community Involvement in City Challenge, A Policy Report*, London: National Council for Voluntary Organisations.

Mackie, Liz (2002), *Putting People at the Heart of the Urban Renaissance*. London: BTEG (Black Training and Enterprise Group) and Urban Forum (November).

Macpherson, W. (1999), *The Stephen Lawrence Inquiry*. London: TSO.

Marshall, Tony F. and others (1997), *Local Voluntary Action Surveys* ('LOVAS') London: Home Office, Research and Statistics Directorate.

Marvin, G.and Guy, M (1997), 'Creating myths rather than sustainability: the transition fallacies of the new localism', *Local Environment*, 2:3

Monbiot, George (2000) 'Breaking point – the smashing of Southampton' in *Captive State, The Corporate Takeover of Britain*. London: Macmillan.

Mooney, G and Danson, M. (1997), 'Beyond 'Culture City': Glasgow as a 'Dual City'' in Jewson, N and MacGregor, S., *Transforming Cities*. London: Routledge.

Nash, Victoria and Christie, Ian (2003), *Making Sense of Community*, London: Institute for Public Policy Research (IPPR) (February).

National Council for Voluntary Organisations (1998), *Research Quarterly No 2*. London: NCVO (June).

National Council for Voluntary Organisations/DETR (2000), *Best Value, A Guide for Voluntary Organisations*, London: NCVO.

Neighbourhood Renewal Unit (2001), *Neighbourhood Renewal Community Chests*. London: DTLR (October).

Neighbourhood Renewal Unit (2001), *Accreditation Guidance for Local Strategic Partnerships*. London: DTLR (October).

Neighbourhood Renewal Unit (2001), *Community Empowerment Fund, Preliminary Guidance*. London: Neighbourhood Renewal Unit.

Neighbourhood Renewal Unit (2001), *Neighbourhood Renewal Community Chests*. London: Neighbourhood Renewal Unit.

Neighbourhood Renewal Unit (2001), *Neighbourhood Renewal, Skills & Knowledge Programme*, London: Neighbourhood Renewal Unit.

Neighbourhood Renewal Unit (2002), *Change in Neighbourhoods, Changing Lives, The Vision for Neighbourhood Renewal*, London: Neighbourhood Renewal Unit.

Northern Ireland Voluntary Trust (1999), *Building Community Infrastructure*, Belfast: Northern Ireland Voluntary Trust (October).

ODPM (2002), *Sustainable Communities: Delivering Through Planning*. Planning policy statement. London: ODPM (July).

ODPM (2002), *Making the System Work Better – Planning at Regional and Local Levels*. London: ODPM.

ODPM (2002), *Living Places – Cleaner, Safer, Greener*. London: ODPM (October).

ODPM (2002), *The Learning Curve*. London: ODPM, Neighbourhood Renewal Unit (October)

ODPM (2002), *The Importance of Tenant Management Organisations in Developing Sustainable Communities*. London: ODPM (November) (summary at: www.housing.odpm.gov.uk/signpost/iss014/07.htm)

ODPM (2003), *Sustainable Communities: Building for the Future*. London: ODPM (February).

Okehampton Locality Group (2002), *Response to West Devon Community Plan*. Okehampton: Okehampton Locality Group (August).

OPM (Office for Public Management) (1999), *Living in Consort and Friary Wards, A Community Survey*. London: OPM and Southwark Council.

Palmer, Guy and others (2002), *Monitoring Poverty and Social Exclusion 2002*, York: Joseph Rowntree Foundation.

Performance and Innovation Unit (Later Strategy Unit) (2002) *Social Capital, A Discussion Paper*. London: Cabinet Office.

Prime, Duncan and others (2002), *Active Communities: Initial Findings from the 2001 Home Office Citizenship Survey*. London: Home Office (Research, Development and Statistics Department) (April).

Plymouth Community Partnership (2002) *Local Social Capital Pilot Project Final Evaluation Report*, Plymouth: Plymouth Community Partnership (September).

Putnam, Robert (2000), Bowling alone: *The Collapse and Revival of American Community*. New York: Simon and Schuster; see also *Social Capital and the World Bank*, http://www.worldbank.org/poverty/scapital/bank1.htm

Putnam, Robert (2001), 'Social capital measurement and consequences', *Isuma* (US) 2:1, Spring (ISSN 1492-0611).

Rahman, Mohibur and others (2001), *Monitoring Poverty and Social Exclusion 2001*. York: Joseph Rowntree Foundation.

Reich, Robert B., (2002), *The Future of Success*, London: Vintage.

Rethinking Construction (2001), *Rethinking the Construction Client*, London: Department of Trade and Industry.

Richardson, Liz and Mumford, Katherine (2002), 'Community, neighbourhood and social infrastructure' in John Hills and Julian Le Grand, *Understanding Social Exclusion*, Oxford: OUP.

Robson, Brian and others (1994) *Assessing the Impact of Urban Policy*. London: HMSO.

Robson, Brian (2000), 'Key challenges for the Urban White Paper', *Cityscape* (newsletter of the ESRC Cities competitiveness and cohesion programme). Liverpool: European Institute for Urban Affairs, Liverpool John Moore University (Autumn).

Rogers of Riverside, Lord (Chair) (1999), *Towards an Urban Renaissance, Report of the Urban Task Force*. (Executive summary.) London: DETR (now ODPM) (June).

Rogers, Richard and Power, Anne (2000), *Cities for a Small Country*. London: Faber and Faber.

Social Exclusion Unit (2002), *Making the Connections: Transport and Social Exclusion Interim Findings*. London: Cabinet Office (May).

Social Exclusion Unit (1998), *Bringing Britain Together: A National Strategy for Neighbourhood Renewal*, London: The Stationery Office, Cm4045, September.

Social Exclusion Unit (2001), *A New Commitment to Neighbourhood Renewal, National Strategy Action Plan*, London: Cabinet Office, January.

Standing Conference for Community Development (2001), *Strategic Framework for Community Development*. Sheffield: SCCD (May).

Taylor, Marilyn (2000), *Top Down meets Bottom Up: Neighbourhood Mangement*. York: Joseph Rowntree Foundation.

Thomas, David N., (1995), *Community Development at Work, A Case of Obscurity in Accomplishment*. London: Community Development Foundation.

Transport 2000 (2002), *Transport and Social Exclusion* (briefing paper). London: Transport 2000.

Tuffrey, M., (1998), *Valuing Employee Community Involvement, Practical Guidance on Measuring the Business Benefits from Employee Involvement in Community Activity*, London: The Corporate Citizenship Company.

Twelvetrees, Alan, (2002), *Community Work*. Basingstoke: Palgrave (third edition).

URBED (Urban and Economic Development group) (2002), *Towns and Cities, Partners in Urban Renaissance. Project Report*, London: ODPM (October/ November). (Accompanying reports in the series are: *Partner Profiles; Case Studies; Workshops Report; Breaking Down the Barriers Report)*.

Walker, David (2002a), *In Praise of Centralism: A Critique of the New Localism*. Catalyst Forum (October).

Walker, David (2002b), 'A lot of local difficulties', *Guardian Society*, 18 Nov.

Waring, Marilyn (1988), *If Women Counted*. London: Macmillan (later republished as *Counting for Nothing*).

Williams, C. and Windebank, J. (1999), *A Helping Hand, Harnessing Self-Help to Combat Social Exclusion*, York: York Publishing Services on behalf of the Joseph Rowntree Foundation

West, A., (2001), *The LSP Guide, A Handy Guide to Getting Involved for Voluntary and Community Groups*, London: Community Development Foundation and the Urban Forum.

Young, Stephen (2000) 'Participation strategies and environmental politics' in Jerry Stoker, Ed., *The New Politics of British Local Governance*, London: Macmillan.

Zahno, Kamila and KENTE (1997), *Working with the Black Voluntary Sector, Good Practice Guide*. London: Pan London Community Regeneration Consortium (c/o London: British Associaton of Settlements).